WIRE
JEWELLERY

WIRE JEWELLERY

Hans Stofer

A & C BLACK

LONDON

First published in Great Britain in 2006
A & C Black Publishers Limited
38 Soho Square
London W1D 3HB
www.acblack.com

ISBN-10: 0-7136-6634-X

ISBN-13: 78-07136-66342

CIP Catalogue records for this book are available from the British
Library and the U.S. Library of Congress.

Book design by Jo Tapper
Cover design by Sutchinda Rangsi Thompson
Copyedited by Rebecca Harman
Project Manager: Susan Kelly
Index: Kevin James
Editorial Assistant: Sophie Page

Printed and bound in China by C&C Offset Printing Co., Ltd.

A & C Black uses paper produced with elemental chlorine-free pulp,
harvested from managed sustainable forests.

Frontispiece:
Collection of Rings by Hans Stofer
Left: Wedding Rings (blackened steel)
Top right: Specimen (blackened steel, glass, wasp)
Bottom right: Venus (blackened steel, silver, pearl)

Contents

Introduction   7

1. An historical perspective   8

2. Wire jewellery today   16

3. The tools of the trade   21

4. Working with wire   30

5. Exercises exploring wire and its potential   50

6. Wire artists   64

Glossary   106

Suppliers   109

Places to view wire jewellery   110

Bibliography   111

Index   112

Acknowledgements

I would like to thank everybody who has shown an interest in this project and to all the jewellers and collections who have so kindly provided photographs and information for this book. In particular I would like to thank the Swiss-born, Munich-based jeweller, Professor Otto Kuenzli for his support and generosity in sharing his knowledge and contacts. Through him I met Dr Ellen Maurer, Curator of the Neue Sammlung, Pinakothek der Moderne in Munich and Frau Bauer from the Danner Stiftung, also in Munich, who gave up their invaluable time to guide me through their collections as part of my research and gave me permission to use images of their work in this publication.

Many thanks as well to Patrick Letschka who helped me with the photography of technical processes and the visual documentation of the individual projects; to Michael Hurley for his suggestions on primary source materials; to Jane Morpeth for her invaluable editorial assistance; to Dr Marjan Unger for being a patient listener, advisor and moral supporter; and Camberwell College of Arts for providing much needed research funds.

I would like to apologise to all the people I bored to death with this project but who nevertheless remained supportive and encouraging with a good dose of British humour, especially Caroline, Thomas and Eloise. And my appreciation to Aphra the cat, for distracting me, for patiently remaining by my side and for listening to my frustrated mutterings when things did not work out.

Finally, a big thank you to Linda Lambert and A&C Black Publishers for giving me the opportunity to get my teeth into this project and to broaden my knowledge and understanding of wire jewellery.

Introduction

Wire has hidden potential as an expressive material, particularly when used to make jewellery. Increasingly people turn to craft activities in order to balance their busy working lives in a meaningful way. Using our hands is comforting and allows us to keep in touch with ourselves, and with what is real. Making jewellery is an activity that addresses both our personal needs and desires, and those of other people around us. The strength and beauty of jewellery lies in this duality of the personal and the public.

For anyone interested in jewellery-making, wire is the ideal material to begin with. Not only is wire an immediate, versatile material, but it offers the possibility of quick results realised relatively easily and cheaply. Ideas can rapidly take shape as a piece of jewellery, through the use of simple hand tools and equipment.

This book will explore the nature and possiblities of wire as a material, as well as covering tooling, equipment, simple jig making and formers, the manipulation of wire, and the detailing and finishing of pieces. The tools, processes and other equipment featured in this book encompass a broad range of approaches to jewellery-making using wire. Obviously all the tools, equipment and processes discussed are part of the jewellery trade, but whilst they are useful for successfully making wire jewellery, the knowledge and skills gained can also be applied to making other metal objects.

A brief historical and contextual background is provided, supported by images of work by makers and artists who have used wire as part of their jewellery and who have helped to shape this relatively young genre. It was not my intention to produce a comprehensive survey of wire-jewellery artists and makers today. The selection of work in this book is entirely personal and based on my experience and contacts with designer-makers who have worked with or used wire at some point in their careers to express their ideas and concepts. Whilst I am aware that this selection is necessarily limited, I nevertheless hope that you find what is presented here both informative and inspiring.

Hans Stofer, 2005

Hans Stofer, *Cherry*, ring, 1994. Steel, welded and blackened.
Collection: Danner Stiftung, Pinakothek der Moderne, Munich.

1.

An historical perspective

A brief history of metals

Metals form a large part of the planet on which we live: we are, quite literally, surrounded by metals. In fact, 80 out of the 103 known elements listed in the Periodic Table are metals. Metals have defined historical eras such as the Bronze and Iron Ages, and played an important part in the evolution and development of civilisations. Metal artefacts helped to shape human environments and habitats, rituals and cultures.

It is believed that the metalworking tradition started almost simultaneously throughout the world between 5000-4500 BC. Initially, mining processes were basic and efforts at smelting only produced small amounts of pure metal – just enough to produce protective ornaments but not sufficient to make tools, weapons or small vessels.

According to the British Museum, some of the earliest metal man-made objects are copper; they were found in Turkey and date from c.5000 BC. The Mesopotamians were among the first peoples to use copper to produce adornments. The Vinca copper culture emerged in former Yugoslavia around 4500 BC, and at roughly the same time the Egyptians were experimenting with copper alloys such as bronze. Other examples of metalworking in ancient cultures include items made of gold, silver, copper and later bronze, found in different parts of the world. Metal was mostly used for tools and weapons – implements which made the daily tasks of hunting and fighting wars easier and more effective – as well as personal ornaments. With the development and evolution of metalworking, particular objects and materials acquired new status and significance.

Gold is still regarded as one of the most precious materials. In ancient cultures, gold was considered the most valuable metal, associated with purity, majesty, divinity, and the sun. It is incorruptible, neither rusting like steel nor tarnishing like silver, and as such has often been linked with the highest inspiration of the spirit. As the sun never dies, so the Ashanti believe that gold symbolises immortality. For example, on the golden stool of the Ashanti state the gold is a symbol of the sun and its energy, which is vital for life, and in particular of their king's power, well-being and longevity.

The ancient Chinese put gold into the mouths of the dead before burial. In many ancient cultures – including those of China, Japan and Egypt – gold was diluted and drunk in the belief that it would prolong life. These elixirs were distributed via the main trade routes of the ancient world. In ancient Japan the tree of life was believed to have had a golden trunk and golden branches. The golden apples of the Nordic heaven, Asgard, were believed to prevent the gods from growing old. Even in medicine today, gold is sometimes used and injected as treatment for severe arthritis.

In Western classical tradition, silver was linked with Jupiter, who created the second age of mortals, the Silver Age. Because of its delicate colour, silver was associated with purity, femininity and the moon, and alchemists believed that silver related to the lunar, female energies.

Although silver was considered less precious than gold, it too was regarded as a divine material with life-prolonging powers. Ancient Chinese alchemists prescribed elixirs containing silver to help the drinker achieve immortality, and the ancient Egyptian gods were said to have silver bones. It has long been known that water carried in silver flagons stays fresh for longer than in containers made from other materials. Settlers travelling though the American West used to purify containers of water by leaving silver dollars in the water overnight. Today there is a resurgent interest in homeopathic medicine in colloidal silver as a remedy for combatting colds and viruses. Silver's antiseptic properties are also used in skin-care creams and skin-healing plasters. However, the traditional medical community is still wary of accepting the gentle healing power of colloidal silver as a natural antibiotic, as science has yet found no explanation for its efficacy.

The healing and spiritual powers of metals have, throughout history, been fully exploited by priests and medicine men. In China, for example, traditional acupuncture made use of metal needles. Acupuncture is a system of holistic healing discovered and developed in China and other countries in the Far East, which has been used for over 2000 years (some say perhaps even 5000 years). The principal aim of acupuncture is to treat the whole person, inserting gold-tipped needles into key positions on the human body, in order to re-establish the equilibrium between the physical, emotional and spiritual in the body, and to unblock the flow of energy.

Whilst gold and silver were generally reserved for kings and the ruling classes, copper and bronze were much more readily available and tended to be used by the broader population for domestic ware, tools, weapons and for cheaper versions of adornments for everyday use. Different metals were often associated with different castes, particularly amongst the nomadic warrior tribes from the Far East up to Central Asia. For example, steel was the metal of the warriors, silver was the metal of the medicine man, and gold was the metal of kings, as the kings were the mortal representatives of the gods. Within many different cultures, the social and political significance of particular metals altered over time, as the wealth and trading connections of these various societies inevitably fluctuated through the ages.

The technique of smelting iron was discovered in Mesopotamia around 1200 BC by the warrior Hittites. Iron was a metal that had been recognised for thousands of years and was much more plentiful than copper; however, it was considered inferior to copper as it rusted. Ancient Middle Eastern civilisations gradually developed iron into the most useful metal as they learnt to work it, forging weapons, tools, chariots and other significant and functional items. But the methods and processes involved in creating objects from iron were extremely laborious and limited to forging alone, and it took the Indo-European civilisation another 2500 years to learn to cast iron. Interestingly, the Chinese had mastered iron casting much earlier.

With the discovery of iron and steel, the quality and strength of weapons, domestic ware and tools improved dramatically. Whilst gold and silver have remained precious and rare, steel is now one of the most commonly used materials in architecture, industry and design. Iron and steel played only a minor part in traditional jewellery-making until the end of the 18th and beginning of the 19th centuries, because (unlike gold and silver) they were generally associated with tools and weapons. Steel is also more difficult to process and manipulate than gold, silver and copper, and it rusts (which is obviously an undesirable quality, particularly when producing adornments).

However, cut steel (brightly polished steel studs fastened to steel plates) was a popular component for all manner of jewellery from the 17th century onwards. British jewellers exported this popular commodity to France, Italy, Prussia, Spain and Russia. There are also some beautiful examples of iron jewellery manufactured and sold in early 19th-century Germany to support the fighting of the Prussian War of Liberation against Napoleon. Such work made during that period is known as 'Berlin' jewellery. Originally produced by Prussian foundries from molten iron, pieces were cast from models made in brass or silver then cleaned, polished and lacquered to a matt finish. Separate units were rejoined and linked together with fine wire. After Napoleon defeated Prussia he looted the foundries, stealing moulds and technical information so that he could have iron work produced in the foundries of Paris.

Metals are divided into two major classifications: ferrous and non-ferrous. The first group identifies all metals and alloys which contain iron. Those without iron content fall into the latter group, and these metals are divided into three further subgroups: precious, base and alloy metals.

Gold, silver and platinum are part of the precious group whilst copper, lead and zinc are considered base metals. Precious and base metals are used to create alloys such as bronze, brass and pewter. The mixing of metals changes the melting point of the alloy either upwards or downwards. These properties are used as part of the casting process and to create solders (alloys used for joining metals using heat).

In ancient civilisations (such as those of the ancient Chinese, Egyptians, Nubians, Greeks and Celts) casting and forging were the most commonly used processes in the production of utensils, weapons and ornaments. Cast ingots, sheets or rods were split with a chisel into thin strips then either twisted, rolled or forged into thin wires in preparation for making springs, spirals, loops and links for adornments.

Jewellery could be purely decorative or could be worn for its protective powers or functionality. The fibula, as worn by the ancient Greeks, Romans and Celts, for example, was a brooch designed to secure clothing as well as to fulfil a decorative, ornamental purpose. During the Iron Age in Mesopotamia (now Iran) and later across the ancient Near East, thin, split, forged, folded and flat coiled silver wire brooches were used as currency. Whole pieces or broken-off segments were valued according to their equivalent weight and exchanged for goods.

In South-East Africa there was a similar tradition of using metal in the form of rods or forged bars for currency right up to the beginning of the 20th century. For example in south-eastern Nigeria, long, bent, thick copper and brass wire rods, known to Europeans as 'Calabar Bars', were used in local trade as currency until as late as 1910. Metals are sacred in many African countries because they are rare, valuable, strong, long-lasting and associated with gods; some believe that the shinier a metal is the more power it contains. Some European traders used wire rods as currency when trading in various areas of Africa.

A brief history of wire

Today wire can be bought in various gauges, alloys and shapes ranging from round to square, or can be made by drawing (pulling) rods through the tapered holes of a drawplate. This technique of shaping wire using drawplates was first invented in Persia during the 6th century AD, but did not reach Europe until the 10th century AD as most of the processes involved were closely-guarded artisan-family secrets. In 1564 the German inventor Rudolf von Nurnberg developed a water-driven machine which helped to increase wire production.

In Europe, wire became a cheap raw material at the beginning of the 19th century due to the Industrial Revolution. With the invention of special machines, it was possible to manufacture different-gauged wire in large quantities at affordable prices. Mild steel wire was galvanised (the process of applying a zinc coating to fabricated steel material by immersion into a bath of molten zinc) with tin to prevent it from rusting. This type of wire is today commonly used for fencing or as binding wire in gardening.

Thin forged strands of laminated iron were first used as a material for repairing broken glass or ceramic items in 17th-century rural Slovakia, as it was a cheap and simple way for the poor to repair their broken domestic ware. Those who travelled the villages repairing broken glass and ceramic ware with wire became known as 'tinkers'. Slowly this form of wire work developed into a trade and the tinkers established themselves as genuine professionals. By the late 19th century, tinned wire and a set of pliers were the basic tools of the trade for tinkers as they travelled the cities and villages. Their skills and inventiveness were renowned and much appreciated; they were able to repair, using only wire and their craft skills, glass jars and bottles so that they were absolutely watertight. Today we would use glue or throw the broken item away, whereas in those days such objects were much more difficult to replace. At annual Easter gatherings in parts of Bavaria, Bohemia and Slovakia during the Austro-Hungarian Empire, competitions were organised where tinkers could prove and display their skills. They would be asked to wrap up an uncooked egg in wire in the most elaborate and ornamental way without breaking the shell. These were regarded as feats of skill rather than of artistic expression.

At the beginning of the 20th century, the craft of wire-working reached its height with nearly ten thousand tinkers operating in Europe and America. In addition to repair work, tinkers were often commissioned to produce household goods such as fruit bowls, whisks and newspaper stands from wire. The results were often unique, innovative and very beautiful. Before long, there was such demand for household goods made of tinned steel wire that small wire workshops emerged in Europe and the USA in order to increase production to feed the growing demand. At this stage, most of the objects were still produced by hand as skilled manpower was readily available. Hand-making also allowed greater versatility and adaptability in the range of products created.

With the invention of stainless steel and plastics, these beautifully crafted wire objects started to lose their popularity and production came to a near standstill by the end of the 1930s. With the decline of the market and the closing of the workshops, an invaluable wealth of knowledge and expertise disappeared. During its heyday, wire-working produced a great variety of items, rich in ingenuity and beauty despite being made with very little, but driven by pure skill and creativity.

The beginnings of contemporary wire jewellery

Since the beginning of the 20th century, there has been a renewed interest in and appreciation of non-precious types of materials such as brass, copper and steel wire. The rediscovery of the ordinary and mundane has produced some of the most innovative and challenging work, both in the fields of the fine and the applied arts. Boundaries have been broken down and the floodgates opened for a more inclusive, interdisciplinary way of working.

The use of more common materials marked the beginning of what we now call 'art jewellery'. Materials are chosen for their ability to express concepts and to challenge perceptions; ideas and expression, rather than simply the materials, determine the value of a piece.

The Victoria and Albert Museum in London houses some stunning steel wire jewellery made between 1890 and 1900 by the British sculptor Sir Alfred Gilbert. Gilbert, who is possibly most famous for the creation of the bronze statue 'Eros' in Piccadilly Square in London, enjoyed making jewellery throughout his career as a sculptor. Another sculptor who raised the status and credibility of wire in the 20th century was the American, Alexander Calder. Calder is famous for his wirework, his beautifully poetic mobiles and stabiles. Stabiles are abstract, completely (or almost completely) stationary sculptural works Calder invented, quite distinct from his other invention, the suspended free-floating sculptures he termed 'mobiles'.

Since Calder, there have not been many artists and designers who have been able to match his prodigious inventiveness using a material which was generally considered basic and mundane. Calder had intuitive understanding of this material and its artistic potential. He produced a huge number of objects – sculptures, portraits, mobiles, stabiles and jewellery – in wire. Wire was his artistic language.

Calder's wire jewellery and some of his small-scale mobiles and objects were not made for mass consumption. They were made for family and friends as gifts and tokens of his affection. Often he would make these wire creations on the spot using only simple hand tools and found objects. Reputedly he never travelled anywhere without a reel of wire and a set of pliers. The immediacy and low-technical means required in wireworking suited his manner of thinking and his temperament. Successful objects made in wire are the result of a sharp, practical and logical mind, a flair for problem solving and improvising. In this respect Calder was not unlike the Eastern European tinkers who, in earlier centuries, had travelled the continent making their repairs using only wire and simple hand tools.

There is a carefree, almost whimsical, but highly sensitive and poetic quality to Calder's jewellery which is full of life and innovation. This may well be because he was in fact an untrained jeweller, but one who had a gift for enjoyment and adventure. As a trained engineer he showed a clear and logical approach to the continuous line, structure and volume of his material. Working with wire requires analytical thinking, planning, spatial awareness and confidence. It is like painting with watercolours; each mark has to be right, there and then. Mistakes or inaccuracies are immediately visible and impossible to repair.

Calder can be seen as the true father of contemporary wire jewellery, offering his very personal, abundant solutions to the field of adornment. Through his work he created a platform for others to build on and pushed the material and its applications to previously untested limits. He paved the way for others to follow, to enjoy and to share the beauty of wire and all its hidden potential.

2

Wire jewellery today

The quality of outstanding work in wire manifests itself in the treatment of the detail. There is little room in wirework to disguise mistakes. Imperfections become more obvious when using limited means like wire and simple hand tools. Each and every move will be visible and noticed. This is why it is important to plan and think ahead while you are working the wire. Preparation of the material and appropriate use of tools and formers are both essential factors in producing quality work.

Today there is a wide range of interesting wire jewellery produced in sweatshops in India and on street markets, which may look fine at first glance. Some pieces might well be beautifully finished; others, however, are more likely to be less refined or even outright crude. If we inspect some of these wire objects more closely, we may discover that the cut-off ends are often left raw. Insufficient time spent on refining sharp ends can be dangerous for the wearer or may damage fabrics.

Whilst I advocate popularising craft skills and making them accessible to a broader audience, I do have my reservations about the quality of finishing and detailing of some of the goods offered for sale in market stalls or alternative shops. I believe that it would not take much time or effort to address and resolve these problems. A consideration for detail and finishing must be taken seriously as that forms an integral, vital part of the creative process. Ultimately it is the small details that help to make a piece of jewellery great.

The raw materials

Physical and mechanical properties define one metal from another. These properties and qualities are determined, like all matter, by the internal atomic structure and order of the material. Some metals will corrode or tarnish; some will remain unaffected by acids, air or other external influences.

Most metals can be polished. The effect achieved by polishing is called lustre. The hardness of the material determines the degree of lustre or polish possible.

Some metals polish better than others; for example, silver and copper can be polished to a mirror-like finish, whereas gold and platinum polish less well.

The malleability of metal allows us to bend, twist or compress it, whereas its ductility means that we are able to draw, roll and stretch it into sheets or wire. Drawing and rolling – like hammering, bending and twisting – will rearrange the metal's internal crystalline structure, which means that the manipulated areas will become harder and more difficult to form. In order to prevent the material becoming 'stressed' or overworked, and to prevent it from eventually splitting, we must anneal it regularly.

Annealing

Annealing, or softening metal with heat, is one of the most important processes used as part of the metalworking practice. This is usually carried out with a gas torch or in a kiln. Heating the metal will restore and 'relax' the granular distortion within the material to its original structural form. As a result, the metal softens again and can be reworked. The temperature to which metal is heated and the method of cooling varies with different metals. When metal is heated up it will change colour, ranging from dark brown to a yellow-white, before it starts to melt. Depending on the metal, this visual

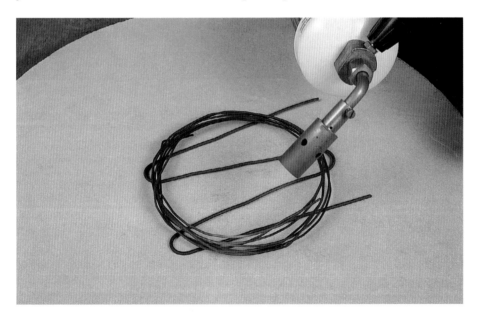

Annealing wire

indicator provides a rough guide to its approximate temperature. It is essential that all parts of the metal are heated evenly. Most metals have reached the annealing stage once their colour reaches cherry red; the exception is platinum, which must be heated until it is white hot.

If the piece to be annealed includes soldered parts, the type of solder used should be assessed prior to heating. The annealing temperature of soldered objects must be lower than the melting point of the solder to avoid the piece falling apart. Soft-soldered pieces, such as those joined with lead solder, cannot be heated up to high temperatures. Lead-based solder will burn into the surface of some precious metals (e.g. silver) when heated beyond its solder temperature. It is also important to ensure that the metal is heated evenly during the annealing process. To prevent wire from melting during annealing, it must be tightly coiled with the ends wrapped around the coil to hold it together. A soft, almost yellow, flame, with very little air should be used to anneal the metal, and then the metal should be left to cool naturally. Most metals, with the exception of copper, will remain hard when quenched in cold water after they have been evenly heated to the annealing temperature.

Preparing to work with wire

Wire is a cheap but versatile material which can be manipulated relatively simply. It can be cut, bent, stretched, drawn, forged, twisted, plaited, coiled, wrapped, knotted, hammered, filed, sharpened, polished, mattened, soldered, welded, clamped, embossed, sand-blasted, etched, heat-treated, patinated, waxed, varnished, plated, painted, enamelled, powder-coated and more.

For anyone beginning to explore the potential and possibilities of wire in jewellery I would suggest working with an annealed, soft wire such as mild steel, copper or brass, rather than hard-drawn, spring wire such as stainless steel or piano wire. Working with hard-drawn and spring wire requires a set of good-quality tools and a slightly different working method. Tougher materials should only be tackled at a later stage once you have acquired more experience and knowledge.

In my own work I tend to use predominately prefabricated annealed wire which I buy in large quantities from a metals' supplier. I prefer to work with the most basic mild steel wire used as binding wire. It is cheap, and it rusts, but it suits my way of working. Someone else might prefer to use the slightly more expensive copper or brass wire as their raw material.

For the production of small quantities of precious metal wire you would, in

Drawing wire down to size

Use a file to taper one end of the wire then, if necessary, anneal wire before applying a fine coat of beeswax to the wire surface as a lubricant. Insert the tapered end of the wire through the conical hole of the drawplate. Push the pointed end of the wire through the hole that is almost the same size as the thickness of the wire.

Please note that the punched numbers on the drawplates mark the front of the tool. Grip the filed end of the wire with either the drawtongs or some serrated parallel pliers and pull straight through the hole. Repeat this for each decreasing hole until the wire is the diameter you want. Also ensure that you occasionally anneal the wire to keep the material soft and malleable, maybe after every two to three pulls.

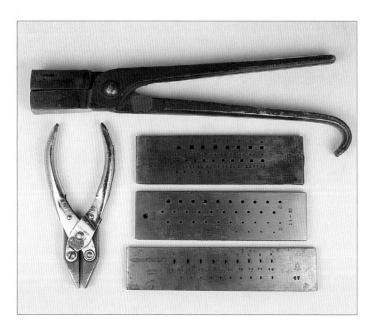

Wire Drawing Tools

These tools are for drawing wire down to size by hand. For thicker wire a drawbench would be essential.
• Hand drawtong
• Parallel pliers
• Drawplates, with holes of various sizes and profiles.

a more traditional jewellery setup, use a rolling mill and drawplates. Hand-operated rolling mills and drawplates are expensive. However, if you intend to work in precious metals it does reduce your investment in materials as you are able to roll down wire in a square wire mill from a few basic gauged metals on demand. The rolled-down square wire can then easily be drawn into round wire to the required size through a drawplate. Rolling mills and drawplates should only be used for precious and non-ferrous metals. The quality of the holes in the drawplate determines the surface quality of the wire. The surface of the wire should be polished if drawn through a good quality, cared-for drawplate. Avoid drawing down any steel and other tough materials as they can permanently damage the holes of the drawplate.

The holes in the drawplate are graduated, as they are used to reduce wire thickness or to change its profile, for example, from round to oval. Clamp the drawplate firmly into a vice before pulling the annealed wire through the appropriate, graduated holes using drawtongs. The drawing wire will lengthen as the metal is compressed when pulled through gradually smaller holes. The wire also hardens and becomes more brittle as it is drawn down. To prevent it tearing, make sure that the wire is occasionally annealed to keep it ductile. Wire thicker than 2 mm in diameter is difficult to draw down by hand. Most traditional jewellers will have a drawbench which makes the drawing down of thicker wire easier. They may also use this piece of equipment to straighten thick wire.

Rolling mills and drawplates are useful but not essential. Today most wires of ferrous, non-ferrous and precious metals can be bought prefabricated from metal merchants or bullion dealers in various sizes and profiles. Working in precious materials can be costly. To test ideas and to avoid any unnecessary wastage I tend to make models in brass or copper wire first. This approach allows me to clarify and resolve my ideas using a cheaper material and helps me assess roughly how much precious material I will need to create the final piece. The model can be weighed and its equivalent weight can be worked out based on the specific density of the materials. For example, a copper model is about half the weight of gold with the density of gold being 19.30 and that of copper 8.89. So, by doubling the weight of the copper model we will know the approximate weight of the final piece in gold.

3

The tools of the trade

As makers our hands are our primary tools. Through them we express ourselves and learn about objects and materials. Using our hands gives us a sense and feel for the potential and limits of the materials we use. This understanding is in judging how to select and best utilise a material or item as part of the creative development of ideas.

Although our hands play an important part when manipulating wire, there will be limits to what we are able to do with our bare hands. That is the point at which we use tools suitable for the wireworking process, such as different sized and shaped pliers, hammers, files, formers and jigs.

Tools have been designed and developed to fulfil very specific tasks. As craftspeople we all have favourite tools we feel comfortable working with. New tools require some time to get used to; it is advisable to put time aside to try them out to see what they are capable of. Tools have their own characteristics, strengths and weaknesses; these need to be utilised as part of the making process.

The selection of hand tools for the wireworker who makes jewellery is relatively small. Good quality tools are not cheap, but purchasing good quality tools will pay dividends in the long run as they will make tasks easier and save you time. In addition to the good-quality tools available in shops, I often buy second-hand tools in flea markets or car-boot sales for the purpose of adaptation. Some tools will be perfect as they are, but others may have to be adapted and customised to perform a more accurate or different task from that which they were created for. For example, some flat pliers have ridges to allow a firm grip and to prevent the wire from slipping away when in use. However, these ridges also leave marks on the surface of the material, so, to prevent any damage to the material, I file these ridges away.

The process of adaptation changes as your ideas and work develop. As part of this development you will discover that, over time, there are tools and implements which you will use more than others. This is all part of standardising your materials and methods. It is not essential to have every single tool or material on offer to produce work of individuality and excellence. In fact, limiting yourself to only the essentials can be an excellent discipline, in that it encourages you to fully explore and exploit the potential of particular tools and materials.

Hand tools are personal and should be cared for in the same way as one looks after one's own hands. For this reason I rarely lend my personal hand tools to anyone, I have had some disastrous experiences where tools have come back completely mutilated through inexpert or careless use. In some cases the damage could be repaired, in others I had to purchase a replacement. Be aware that some tools are irreplaceable, particularly if you have inherited them from someone else or if you have had them for some time. This can be distressing and disruptive to your creative development.

There are guidelines as to how to care and look after small hand tools and larger machinery. However, common sense and appropriate use will almost certainly help to prolong the lifespan of any piece of workshop equipment. Here are some basic rules to use as your guidelines:

1. Use common sense and care for your tools.
2. Always choose the most appropriate for the task; incorrect use can damage the tool and diminish its effectiveness.
3. Choose the most effective tool for the task; for example, use bolt croppers to cut thick wire rather than normal side cutters.
4. Whenever possible use hardened tools; as a rule, tools should always be harder than the material you are working with.
5. Avoid mishandling tools and keep cutting edges and blades sharp. The most severe jewellery-making injuries are caused by blunt instruments.
6. Make sure that files and hammer handles are fitted firmly and securely. Never use files without handles. The tang of files are sharp and may injure your hand if used without a handle.
7. Sharp ends and cutting edges should be covered to prevent any accidents.
8. Tools can break. Most tools are hardened and tempered, which increases their strength but also makes them more brittle. They may splinter or chip if dropped or hit with a hammer.
9. Do not overheat tools which have been tempered, such as pliers, piercing saw blades or drills, as this can affect their strength or ability to cut.
10. Keep your tools and equipment clean and dry. Metal tools (unless chrome plated) will rust if stored in a moist or damp environment. They should, therefore, be kept in a dry place. Always clean tools after they have been used, particularly if they are moist, dirty or full of oil.

Tools and processes for wireworking

Pliers

Metal workers and jewellers have used pliers of one sort or another since the beginning of the tradition of manipulating metal into adornments and other objects. They have, together with the hammer, remained virtually unchanged in their function, purpose and design.

Pliers are essential tools for any jeweller and wireworker. Without them the successful manipulation of wire into detailed and refined objects is virtually

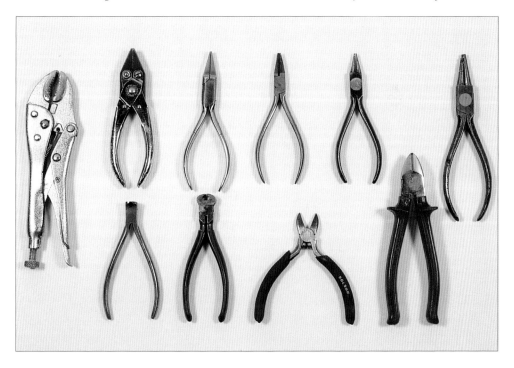

Basic set of pliers which are useful to manipulate various types of wire. For cutting very thick or hard wire you may consider using a metal hacksaw or bolt cutters (not pictured above).

Top row (left to right):
• Mull grips. These pliers can be bought in most ironmongers or plumbers' suppliers.
• Parallel-action pliers.
• Flat-nose pliers.
• Shaped pliers. One side is usually flat, the other rounded. These are particularly useful for bending gentle curves or ring shanks.

• Round-nose pliers. Useful for bending loops and tight curves.
• Round-nose pliers. These have been customised for specific tasks.

Bottom row (left to right):
• Top cutters, for thin wire.
• Top cutters, customised for thin and medium wire.
• Semi-flush cutters.
• Heavy-duty side cutters, for medium and thicker wire.

impossible. Different sized and shaped pliers make it possible to create more intricate and precise forms and patterns using either thin or thick wire. You should always bend simple shapes and bangles in thin materials by hand first, and only use pliers for what cannot be done with bare hands.

There are two types of pliers: parallel-action and pivot-jawed pliers. The jaws of parallel-action pliers always open and close in parallel. Parallel-action pliers are used where a strong grip is required, for example for straightening or drawing wire to size.

The pivot-jaw pliers are only in parallel when closed. They are less suited to a task where a strong grip is needed. There are two basic types of pivot pliers: cross-joint and box-joint. The cross-joint pliers tend to be cheaper and are generally less stable under pressure than the usually better-made box-joint pliers. However, the advantage of pivot-jawed pliers is that they are manufactured with finer jaws, which makes them ideal for bending and manipulating wire and other fine materials.

The jaws of most jewellery pliers are soft and can therefore be filed, shaped or adapted and customised to perform specific tasks.

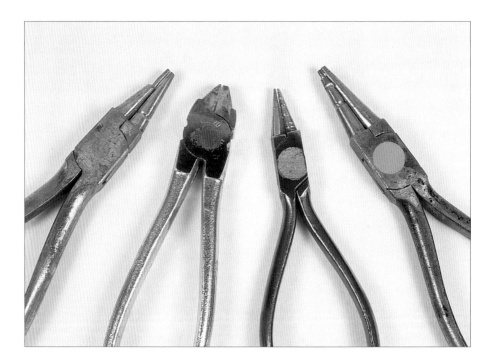

Set of secondhand pliers, which have been shaped to do specific tasks.

Files

Files are very important tools for anyone working in metals or making jewellery. Accurate and effective filing is a key skill if you want to produce quality objects. To achieve good results, your filing, like any other skill, must be carefully practised. Files come in an enormous variety of sizes, profiles and cuts. They are used for cleaning up castings, edges and ends of wires, and for filing flat surfaces and shapes. They cut when pushed forward over the material. To make jewellery you need a basic selection of normal files with handles and a set of smaller needle files. As explained earlier, files without handles are dangerous. Always make sure that the wooden handle fits firmly onto the tang.

As with most tools on the market, the range and quality on offer is diverse. When putting a basic toolkit together, working within a tight budget, it is

Set of useful, basic files.
Files come in different sizes, shapes and cuts (from very fine to coarse).

Top to Bottom:
• Needle files (for small and more intricate detailing): pillar; half-round; square; three square; round.
• Hand files: half-round; crossing; pillar; hand file.

advisable to purchase fewer tools but opt for the best quality you can afford. Good-quality tools last longer, work better and make the manipulation process more enjoyable.

As a Swiss-born maker, I prefer to work with Swiss files. Files made by Valorbe are considered to be the Rolls Royces of files and last for a lifetime, providing of course that you treat and use them appropriately. This is not to say that other makes are not as good. There are a number of other file manufacturers who produce good Swiss-type files.

The coarseness of the Swiss files is numbered from 00 (very coarse) to 6 (very fine). The coarseness of British and American files is defined by name, ranging from rough, bastard and second-cut to smooth and super-smooth. Generally, finer files are more suitable for wire work than coarser ones. The range of shapes and types of files very much depends on the type and scale of work you do.

Hammers and mallets

Metal hammers, raw-hide mallet (used to manipulate metal without damaging the surface) and a jeweller's bench block.

Texturing or flattening wire with a hammer. Always ensure that tools and the bench-block surface are clean.

Piercing saw

The piercing saw is, in addition to files and pliers, probably one of the most useful and essential tools required for jewellery-making. The saw is used for cutting materials, piercing slots, shaping settings and cutting fine patterns into sheet metal. It is also an essential tool for the production of small wire rings and links for chains.

There are various types and sizes of saw frames on the market. Depending on the scale of your work, you may buy a couple of different-sized frames. If you decide to buy only one frame, I suggest that you purchase a fully adjustable piercing-saw frame with a frame depth of approximately 145 mm, constructed from strong metal and with a comfortable wooden handle.

The piercing-saw blades used by jewellers are bought by the dozen and are graded from 8/0s to 0 for fine, and 1 to 14 for coarse. The most commonly used are 2/0s and possibly 4/0s. To ensure that the blades are held firmly, the clamps on either side of the frame should be serrated. The ability to adjust the frame helps to draw the blade taut. It also makes it possible to shorten the frame for the use of any broken blades. Make sure that the blade is inserted correctly with the teeth of the blade pointing towards the handle; in other words, downwards. Tighten the wing nuts by hand, as over-tightening with pliers can damage the thread of the wing nuts. When sawing, as with filing and other jewellery processes, the metal object is traditionally 'clamped' by your hand, with the piece resting firmly on either the bench pin or other work facility. A little bit of beeswax as a lubricant will make the cutting easier and help to extend the lifespan of the blade.

Cutting wire with a
piercing saw.

Cutting rings off
the coil with a
piercing saw.

Jigs

Jigs are mechanical devices designed to hold a component during
manufacturing and to guide the tool. They are predominantly used for the
accurate and repetitive reproduction of standard components in small or
large numbers. In industry, for example, jigs can be very complicated
depending on the form to be clamped and machined. However, jigs do not
have to be complicated. Nails and scrap pieces of wood are often all we need to
build a jig which allows us to bend wire, for example, into equal-sized squares
or an evenly spaced zigzag line. I often use jigs to make multiples, which can
be sold more cheaply than a one-off piece at an exhibition. Of course, jigs can
also be used as part of the making of a unique piece.

Using a simple jig to form repetitive patterns.

Using formers to shape larger rings. Ensure that the formed ends will slightly overlap.

Formers

Formers are tools for giving a coil, winding or curve a required shape, sometimes consisting of a frame or a pin on which the wire can be wound. After the process, the frame or pin will be removed. Over the years I have acquired a range of different formers which I regularly use, made out of different materials including wood, plastics and metals. As with pliers, over time I tend to use a standard set of formers to produce my work. Generally, I prefer to use metal formers. They are stronger and will not give when I have to use a hammer to form the wire around them.

4

Working with wire

Soft, annealed wire purchased in larger reels is often susceptible to kinking. Some people like this aspect and deliberately use these inaccuracies as part of the feel and quality of an object. For me though it is important to use wire which is free of kinks as I want to achieve visual accuracy and precision in my work. The beauty of wire is its immediacy and simplicity; ideas can be transformed and developed quickly into three-dimensional objects.

I spend considerable time on the preparation and planning stage for each piece of work. The preparation of the raw material (wire), the tools and formers is essential if you want to work fluently and without interruption. I often straighten small batches of different-sized wires prior to making. This ensures that I have a stock of prepared materials ready to launch into action when inspiration strikes. Wire is cut from the large coiled reel into standard lengths and then straightened. I also ensure that my pliers are in good working condition and that the right formers are close at hand.

Preparing your own wire

If you do not want to use wire the way it comes from the manufacturer – round in diameter with a shiny surface – you have the option of changing its appearance prior to making your piece. There are some beautiful examples of jewellery pieces where the wire has been manipulated or textured to give the material a more natural and sensual quality. Bundles of wire can be twisted and hammered or wire sections in different metals can be soldered together to form long strips before creating the finished piece. There are endless ways to give your work an individual touch. Some designer-makers will do it through form, texture and content, others may prefer to use wire in its pure manufactured state to express their ideas. As makers we have the opportunity to give meaning to objects in a direct and immediate way. All we need is the confidence to experiment and the ability to trust our creative intuition. With a little experience and determination the rest will follow.

Straightening wire

Straightening batches of wires is a mundane and labour intensive task. I tend to do this job when I am either in between projects or when ideas are flowing less easily. It is sometimes essential to take a break from being creative. Simple manual and repetitive tasks allow ideas to mature subconsciously in their own time whilst your hands and mind are busy concentrating on something else.

There are many ways of ironing out kinks or straightening wire. For example, you can use a simple hand drill, clamp one end of the wire in the vice and the other in the chuck of the drill, then pull and twist it. This method may iron out the kinks but twisting also makes soft wire harder, which can make any subsequent manipulation more difficult. Some jewellers pull their gold, silver or copper wire through two pieces of soft wood. These can either be

Bench vice
Make sure that any vice is firmly clamped to the work bench. I tend to use two ordinary G-clamps to clamp the vice to the table rather than using nuts and bolts. This allows more flexibility in positioning the vice.

31

Straightening wire
After annealing the wire, clamp one end firmly in the vice. Pull and stretch, then unclamp.

pressed together by hand while pulling the wire through or they can be clamped together in a vice.

The most effective way of straightening softened or annealed thin wire is to simply pull and stretch it. You can do this by hand as long as the wire is no thicker than 1-1.2 mm in diameter. You will need a fixed bench or table, a firmly fitted vice, and drawing tongs or pliers which allow you to grip the wire firmly. Clamp one end of the wire into the vice, tightly grip the other end of the wire and pull it towards you as strongly as possible. At some point you should feel the tensioned wire give and stretch a bit. The wire should now be straight. Carefully unclamp the wire from the vice and pliers and cut off the marked ends where the material has been clamped. Store the straightened length horizontally to avoid bending.

Stainless steel and other hardened materials, such as dental wire or titanium, behave in a different way to annealed materials. Hardened or spring metals are alloys designed to resist corrosion or to maintain their form under tough conditions. For example, stainless steel contains chromium (Cr) which prevents the material from rusting. This makes it an ideal material for kitchen utensils such as cutlery and kitchen sinks. The stainless steel used for cutting tools and springs may, in addition to chromium, also contain silicon (Si), vanadium (V) or molybdenum (Mo).

As these metal alloys are tougher than soft annealed metal they require more strength to manipulate them and a slightly different working method. The 'spring back' of hardened or spring wire during the manipulation process is also more prominent than that of the soft annealed metals.It is important to use good-quality tools, as inferior tools will get damaged. It is not possible to straighten stainless-steel wire by pulling, as you can with annealed wire. I either use my hands to iron out bent springy wire or I purchase already-straightened wire (stainless steel welding rod is ideal). Eye protection is, of course, essential.

Bending wire
See '*A little bending exercise*' on pp. 59-62.

Coiling wire
See *Venus Ring* on pp.56-8.
Coils are a trademark feature of wire work. They are beautiful, timeless and full of symbolic meaning. Coiling the ends of wire also serves the purpose of making sharp ends safe in a graceful and stylish way.

Making a perfect loop

1. Cut and straighten annealed wire.

2. File ends flat and de-bur.

3. Grip wire firmly at the end with round-nose pliers.

4. Slowly twist wire, keeping wire as close as possible to the round-nose tips. It is easier to bend if you use more than one action.

5. Centre loop.

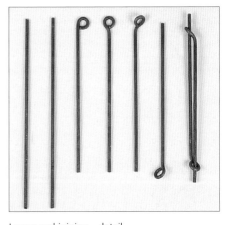

6. Angle loop with parallel pliers if you intend to join two wires together or to create an articulated section where its length can be either extended or decreased.

Loops and joining - detail

Coiling wire - springs, small rings for links and chain links

Remember to wear eye protection during this process.

1. Cut a deep slot into a square sectioned piece of hardwood (beech or similar). The slot should be as deep as possible without slicing the wood in half. The slotted piece of wood is used to hold and guide the wire during the coiling process. If you cannot cut slots then use two flat pieces of wood.
2. Feed one end of the wire through the slot, with enough of the wire sticking out to grip firmly using mull-grip pliers. Clamp wood with wire into vice.
3. Select a straight pin to wrap the wire around. Ensure that the pin is made of either harder or the same material as that you will be coiling.
4. Place pin lengthwise on to wood (lying in same direction as slot).
5. Fold the end of the wire over the pin and clamp both wire and pin with mull-grip pliers.
6. Slowly coil wire. You may occasionally have to adjust the strength of clamping.
7. When you finish coiling, relax your grip to allow the now-tense or sprung-loaded coil to relax before cutting or unclamping the vice.

Mull-grip pliers and wire, preparing for coiling.

Cutting rings off the coil with a piercing saw.

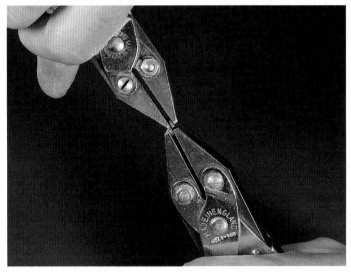

Closing up rings
Grip ring with a pair of parallel or flat-nosed pliers in each hand so that you can still see the open slot. Gently twist one pair of pliers away and the other pair towards you until the open ends meet and are aligned.

Making chains

See Chapter 6 for inspiration, and p. 55 for a chain-making exercise.

Making spirals

Thin wire spirals can be made using only simple pliers and your hands. Use annealed wire. Begin by bending the centre using fine round-nosed pliers. First make a tiny loop then use parallel or flat-nosed pliers to form the spiral.

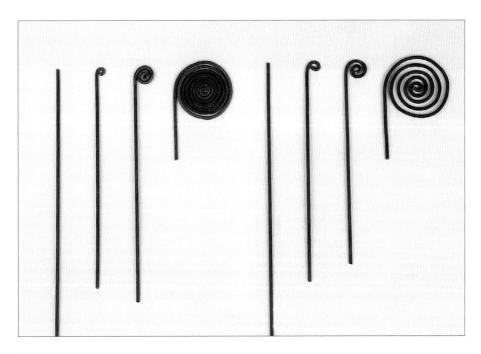

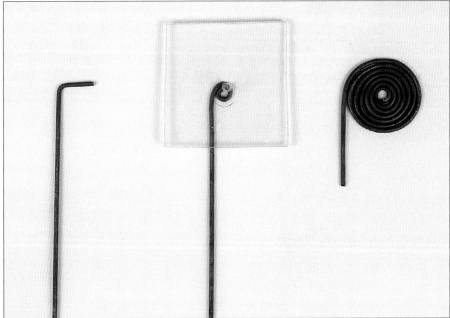

Making a spiral using thick wire.

Making a perfect spiral

1. Drill a hole the same size as the wire diameter into a piece of thick perspex or sheet metal. Bend the end of the wire into a right-angle. Thread wire through hole.

2. Clamp the end of the wire tightly in the vice.

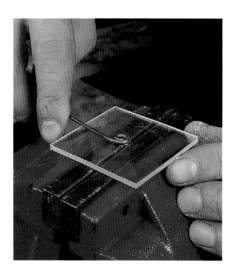

3. Start winding the spiral. The perspex or metal plate acts as a supporting base to ensure that your spiral will be perfectly flat.

Joining wire with wire

Joining wire without soldering or welding is for the purist. The joining methods must be carefully planned and prepared for. One of the most common and effective ways of joining wire is simply twisting the ends of wire strands together. Make sure that these ends are not sharp, and be sure to file them before you twist them together. The twist adds strength and texture and is particularly useful when working with very fine and delicate wire.

There are many other methods of joining wire with wire; some of the most popular are outlined below.

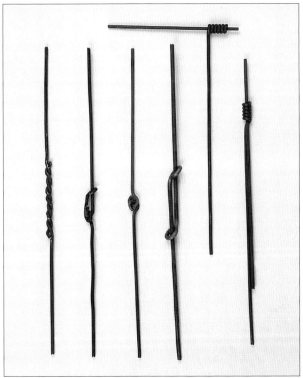

Above:
Joining wire with wire: springs and articulated joints.

Left:
Examples of different ways of joining pieces of wire.

Twisting thin, round wire

Use soft annealed wire. Fold in half, twist loose ends together and clamp firmly into the bench vice. Use a simple hand drill with a simple hook clamped in the chuck to grip and twist the wire. If you do not have a hand drill use a screw driver or another pin-like implement to twist the wire.

Twisting square wire

Anneal, clamp one end into vice and twist the square-sectioned wire using parallel pliers. If you do not want the wire to be damaged, protect wire near the clamping areas with either masking tape or cardboard.

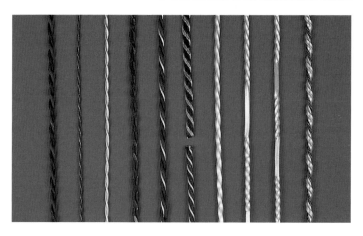

Examples of twisted wire in precious and non-precious metals, showing both round and square section wire.

Soldering

Soldering is one of the most commonly used methods in jewellery-making to join two or more pieces of metal together, and involves joining metals together using flux, solder and heat. It is a particularly useful technique for making wire jewellery.

Most metals can be soldered. It is important to use the appropriate solder and flux for the materials to be joined. Solder is a fusible, lower-melting metal alloy used to fuse the metal sections together. Flux is used to keep the solder joint clean and to prevent oxidisation during the soldering process.

There are two types of soldering: soft soldering and hard soldering. Hard solders are strong and have a high melting temperature. These include gold, silver, copper and brass solder. Soft solders, such as tin alloys, melt at a lower temperature and are generally weaker than hard solders. It is important that the soldering joints are clean and degreased before they are joined together. Dirt and grease can prevent the solder bonding with the metals.

The most commonly used flux for hard soldering is Borax (powdered and mixed with clean water). I use a commercially prepared hard solder paste. Industrial fluxes are more expensive than the traditional Borax cone, but are less likely to 'bubble up' (e.g., raise the solder and parts to be soldered).

Hard solders are divided into three categories, which are defined by their melting points: easy (690°C/1274°F) medium (720°C/1328°F); and hard (740°C/1364°F). These different hard solders are used for different purposes at various stages of the making process. I only use easy solder for repair jobs or extremely delicate work. Everything else I tend to solder with hard solder.

Soft solders are low-melting tin and lead alloys. They are most commonly used in the electronic and building trade, as well as for the production of tin-plated objects. As with hard soldering, solder joints need to be clean and free of grease and an appropriate flux is needed to guarantee a successful solder joint. Soft solders have a very low-melting point (170°C-230°C/338°F-446°F). This makes them comparatively easy to handle. However, soft solder joints are not as strong and durable as hard soldered ones. They should not be used for gold, platinum or silver work - unless you are striving for a particular effect.

Effective soldering depends on the correct use of heat. The flame should be focused, clean and hot enough to bring the metal up to its required soldering temperature. Which soldering torch you choose depends on how often and in what location you do your soldering. Blowtorches are suitable for both hard and soft soldering.

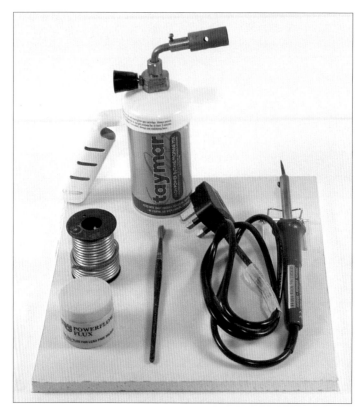

Soft solder equipment:
- Soft solder
- Flux (make sure you use flux which is suitable for the solder)
- Hand torch with propane refill
- Electric solder iron (good for joining fine wire).

Flux, solder and brush for soft soldering.

Traditional jewellers often swear by the mouth blowpipe. However, this requires considerable skill and experience. In my workshop I use a handset connected to a propane gas cylinder with three different sizes of nozzle: fine, medium and large. You do not need an oxygen supply as oxygen is sucked in with the flow of the propane. There are also very effective propane soldering

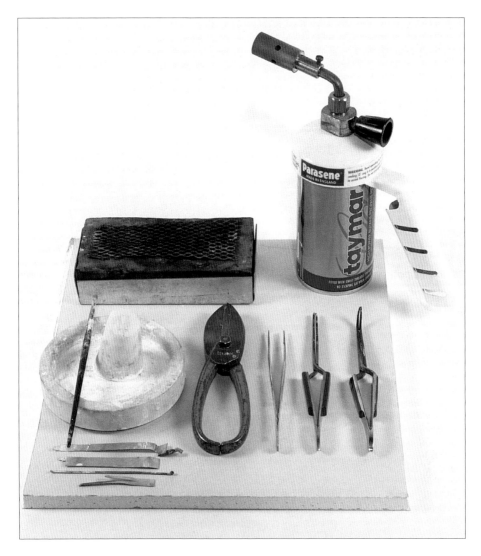

Hard solder equipment:

- Charcoal block with mesh tray. It is easier to control the heat during the soldering process if the work piece is raised. Charcoal absorbs a lot of heat.
- Borax cone (flux) - the most common, general purpose borax. Must be ground with a little clean water in the ceramic borax tray, where it is also traditionally stored. Grind flat end of the cone until a whitish paste is produced.
- Ceramic borax tray
- Brush for applying wet flux paste

- Silver Solder. Clean solder surface, as silver solder will produce a fine patina over time and this can prevent the solder from flowing.
- Hand torch with propane refill
- Jewellers shears (or tin snips) for cutting solder and thin sheet metal. Do not use for wire, as profiled material can damage the cutting edges.
- Steel tweezers, for placing the solder.
- Reverse action soldering pliers, curved and straight. Ideal for clamping parts together during soldering.

torches on the market, with disposable small propane cartridges. They are relatively inexpensive and are very effective, lasting up to ten hours depending on the size and volume of the work. For soft lead soldering of thin wires, you can also use an electrical soldering iron of the sort traditionally used for joining electrical wires.

Spot-welding

Spot-welding is also called resistance welding. The spot-welder is an ideal tool for welding together steel wire and thin sheets of metal. Unfortunately, this joining process is generally not suitable for non-ferrous metals such as copper, brass, silver or gold as these metals are too conductive and therefore tend to melt during the fusing process. However, there has been some research in this area to make resistance welding of precious metals possible using special alloys and electrodes.

There are various types and sizes of spot-welders on the market. Some are fixed, others are portable and hand operated. I use a small portable spot-welder with a timer which can be plugged into a normal single-phase (220/240 V) socket. A welder with a timer is preferable as it allows you to adjust the length and intensity of the current when welding together different-gauged materials.

Spot-welding is an immediate technique and requires relatively little preparation, other than scraping off rust or whipping off grease which may

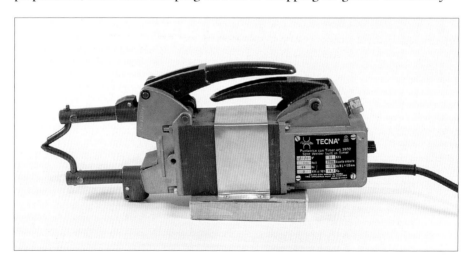

Portable electrical spot welder (Techna) with timer. The timer is essential, especially when working with different gauges of wire. Remember to always wear eye protection.

Simple application of spot-welder for steel wire work.

prevent the fusing process. Two wires or panels of steel are introduced between the two copper electrodes, which the machine can clamp together. Once the trigger is activated, the charge is released and flows through the two electrodes creating a concentrated current where the metal and the electrodes meet. The intensity of the heat created at this point is enough to weld the two wires or plates together. It is advisable to experiment, before starting work, to test the appropriate timer setting and to ensure that the metal has properly fused together.

Surface treatments and finishes

Wire jewellery made from precious metals such as gold and silver often requires little surface finishing due to the nature of the material itself. This is also true for work produced using non-ferrous metals such as copper and brass. Silver, copper and brass do, however, tarnish over a period of time. If you find this feature unattractive then the tarnish can be removed using special metal polish and a soft cloth.

Mild steel, unlike stainless steel, will rust over time. Although some people perceive rust as undesirable and dirty, personally, I love the colour of rust, which is part of the nature of iron and steel. I agree with John Ruskin's statement 'that rust is just so much nobler than pure iron, in so far as it is iron and the air'. He argues that 'in a certain sense, and almost a literal one, we may say that iron rusting is Living; but when pure and polished, Dead.' The colour and texture of rust is beautiful, but can stain the skin or fabric when worn as a piece of jewellery. Rust can be primed, but any substance applied will dull some of its beautiful satin colour.

To prevent or slow down the process of decay we can treat the surface of materials either by making the surface denser by hammering and polishing or by coating it with wax, paint, enamel or a thin coat of metal plate (copper, silver, gold or any other conductive metal).

Polishing wire objects is labour intensive, difficult and can be dangerous if the polishing is done on a polishing machine. Wire work can easily get caught up in the polishing wheel and be damaged. If a polished surface is required, either use already-polished wire or clean up and polish the wire before manipulating it. Make sure that you leave as few marks as possible during the forming process. Remember that any heat treatment will change the colour and surface qualities of the material. If possible, avoid joining methods like soldering or spot welding.

Sandblasting

Sandblasting is a relatively cheap, quick and effective way of cleaning up metal surfaces in preparation for etching, patinating, waxing, painting, powder coating or enamelling. It can also be used to matten surfaces or to apply simple patterns by masking off particular areas prior to sandblasting them.

A jet of abrasive grit or silicon beads is blown from a nozzle under pressure onto the metal, removing any unwanted substances. Treated surfaces can then either be left as they are or they can be blackened, waxed, painted or enamelled.

Etching

Etching is used either to gently roughen up metal surfaces prior to other surface treatments or to apply texture and pattern. Asphalt-based 'stop outs' can be brushed onto metal surfaces to coat certain parts so they will not be etched.

Etched surfaces can be beautiful, but working with acid always has the potential to be dangerous and you must use appropriate acid-proof facilities.

Always ensure that you are working in a well-ventilated area, and that you use adequte protection for your eyes, hands and clothes.

During the etching process the surface of the submerged metal will gradually be broken down and worn away by the diluted acid solution. The piece will diminish in volume depending on the acid type, its strength and the length of time the piece remains submerged in the acid bath. Over time, the acid solution will discolour and become saturated with metal deposits, which makes the solution less effective. Consequently, saturated solutions must be changed occasionally, and they must be disposed of in a safe and appropriate way. Contant your local council for accurate information about solution disposal. Nitric-acid solutions can be flushed down the drain, providing they are diluted with large amounts of water.

For etching metals, the most commonly used acid is nitric acid. Never use pure acid. Pure acid is very powerful and can dissolve your wire in no time. Water-acid solutions vary in proportions, but are usually mixed in a volume of one part acid to two parts water. If you need the solution to be weaker, add more cold water, but be aware that acids react when they come into contact with water. To prevent the acid from spattering when mixing the acid-water solution, always pour acid slowly into cold water. You MUST protect your eyes and hands with safety glasses and gloves, and wear protective clothing!

Spraypainting

If you want to add a touch of colour, spraypainting can be used to finish work. Spraypaint applied with skill and expertise enables you to achieve some unusual and beautiful results. For purists and traditionalists, spraypainting jewellery is a definite no-no. To the conventionally-minded, spraypaint is acceptable on machines, cars and other industrially manufactured goods, but unacceptable as a jewellery finish.

As a trained engineer, I think otherwise. I find spraypaint a wonderfully direct and liberating medium for finishing work. The spraypainting process is a relatively straightforward and immediate finishing process. As long as you ensure that the layers of paint are kept thin, and are left to dry thoroughly inbetween coats, you will quickly achieve a good result.

I often use good-quality car-body spraypaints in aerosol tins to finish my pieces. The pieces are sandblasted first, then primed before I apply thin layers of paint which, after they have dried, I often rub back and then repaint until the final desired effect has been achieved. If I am dissatisfied with a particular finish, I simply sandblast it off and begin again.

Plating

Metal plating is one of the most commonly used surface finishes today. It is a quick and effective process. Objects can be transformed without much effort and at little cost. Most good conductive metals can be plated. Plating is used to enhance the appearance of objects, to apply a protective cover to prevent metals from tarnishing or oxidising, or to enhance resistance to chemicals.

Metal objects are submerged into an electroplating bath. An electric current is passed through a solution containing certain compounds of metals such as gold, silver, copper or chrome. In the process, thin deposits of metals will cling to the surface of the submerged object. The longer an object is kept in the plating bath, the thicker the metal deposit will be.

Enamelling

Enamel is used for decorative or protective purposes and comes in various brilliant colours. As an artistic medium, enamel is loved for its vibrant and expressive colours, its durability and its practical qualities. Enamelling can be traced back to ancient Egypt where the beauty and potential of this colourful glassy substance fused onto metal was developed into a high art. Enamelled jewellery and objects were as treasured and appreciated by people then as they are today.

Enamel is basically glass. It is made up of flux or frit, which is clear glass, and metal oxides, which provide the colour. Variations in the composition of the frit and metal oxide produce enamels with varying viscosity under heat and different hardness and brilliance upon cooling.

As a process, enamelling is relatively simple and easy to master, but to produce work of consistently high quality requires extensive knowledge and experience. Enamel powder is applied onto a gummed metal surface. The powdered object is then fired in a kiln until the enamel powder melts.

Enamels are divided into four groups: opaque, translucent, transparent and opalescent. Opaque enamels will allow no light through, translucent will allow some, transparent a lot and opalescent will vary in translucency and opacity.

Traditionally, good-quality enamels came in chunks of glass crystals which had to be crushed, ground into fine powder and washed before they were applied to metal. Today most enamels and accessories can be purchased prefabricated and ready to use.

Enamel is applied by dusting using a fine sieve. It is essential to coat the metal with a prepared gum (arabic, tragacanth) solution to ensure that the enamel dust will stick to the metal before the piece is fired.

Enamel can also be used like paint. Painted enamel is called Limoges (after the French town where it originated). To paint enamel onto metal, it should first be ground to a powder-like consistency. A drop of lavender oil is added as a binder and to make the application onto metal easier. The individual colours can be blended, but this should be done in successive firings to prevent the colours running into each other.

Stove enamelling

Fridges, dishwashers, cookers and radiators are stove enamelled. Stove enamelling is an industrial process where a type of enamel is made heat proof by treatment in a stove. Paint-like enamel is sprayed onto the metal surface and then fired. You can get almost any shade of colour, just as with spraypaint. The advantage of stove-enamelled surfaces is that they are more permanent than paint and more resilient to scratches. The disadvantages are that you need to find a specialist company who is prepared to surface treat small-scale work to your standards, and who will have the colour you want. This leaves less room for experimentation - unless you have a large wallet!

Patination and oxidation

A large number of metals will naturally form a film of oxide on their surface. This chemical reaction is the reason the colour and texture of metals change over time. Mild steel will turn rusty (orange to brown), silver will tarnish (yellow to black) and copper and bronze will turn either black or turquoise green if exposed to rain or salt water. This change of state in metal is called patination.

The natural patination of metals can be accelerated with the use of specific chemicals. Chemically patinated surfaces are often very beautiful, but they may not necessarily be permanent. The use of chemicals is also dangerous and must only be carried out in well-ventilated areas, preferably using purpose-built fume cabinets. If you are interested in further exploring this subject, you should consult *The Colouring, Bronzing and Patination of Metals* by Michael Rowe and Richard Hughes (Watson-Guptill Publications, New York, 1991).

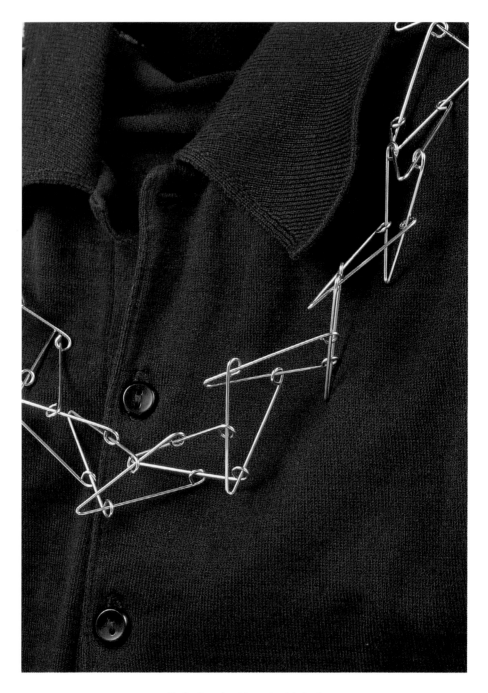

Hedgehog (necklace, dental steel)
This necklace is very light and springy. Its character is soft but spiky. *Hedgehog* really kicked off my interest and passion for working with wire. (See page 51)

5

Exercises exploring wire and its potential

For the following exercises I used predominantly annealed mild steel wire, purchased in large reels from a steel merchant, and dental steel wire (a type of medical stainless steel used by dentists). Dental steel is slightly softer and easier to manipulate than ordinary stainless steel. These are materials which suit my way of working. You may prefer to use non-ferrous or precious metal wire instead. Naturally, these materials will be easier to manipulate than mild, stainless or dental steel.

The exercises presented in this chapter serve as basic starting points for you to develop, reinterpret, customise and improve on.

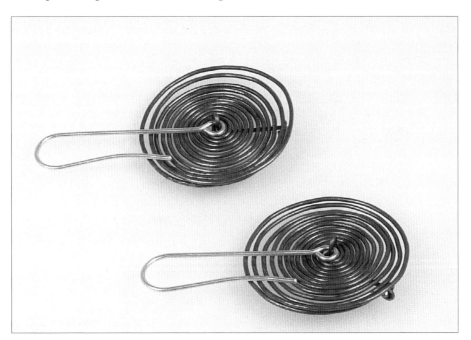

Orbit earrings (silver, mild steel)
(See page 53)

Hedgehog Necklace (dental steel)

(See photograph, p. 50)

1. Use 1.2 mm (¹/₁₆ in.) thick round wire, not too soft if you are using non-ferrous metal.
2. To make a necklace without a clasp, cut 35 lengths of 104 mm (4 in.) pieces.
3. Use a flat hand file to flatten all the ends and remove the burs.
4. Use round-nose pliers to bend equal loops at either ends. The loops must face in the same direction and be aligned (see picture below).
5. Use a fine waterproof marker to mark out the centre of the each piece.
6. Use flat-nose pliers to bend all links to create a wedge shape of about 60° so that the loops face inwards. Align the links so they lie flat.

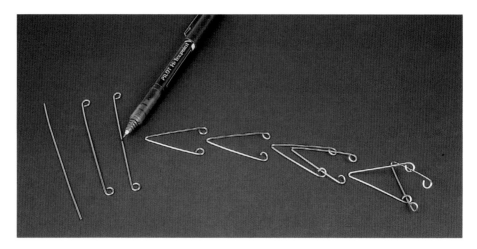

7. Use either flat-nose pliers or parallel pliers to open up all the loops identically so a 1.2 mm (¹/₁₆ in.) thick wire can be passed through the slots.
8. Using either flat-nose pliers or parallel pliers, connect the links by opening and closing the links. Make sure that the individual links are connected from the same side and that the points are always facing in the same direction.

Orbits Earrings (mild steel, silver)

Also see 'Making Spirals' (p. 36) and photograph p. 51

To make the orbit shapes:
1. Use 0.6 mm annealed wire, either mild steel or another non-ferrous metal of your own choice.
2. Cut two lengths of 800 mm (31 in.).
3. Straighten both lengths in a vice.
4. Grip one end of the straightened wire with flat-nose pliers and bend tightly to form a U-shape. Repeat on the second wire.
5. Use either flat-nosed or parallel pliers to grip about 5 mm (1/5 in.) of the curved end of the U-bend and bend the shorter end down 90°.
6. After you have bent down the shorter part, keep hold of the wire and use the long part to start forming the spiral using your free hand.
7. Once you have completed the spiral to the size you want, repeat the same process to form the second spiral.
8. When you have finished the spirals, carefully bend down the short wire of the U-bend so it lies flat on the spiral.
9. Cut back the spiral ends with side- or top-cutters as far as the bent-down wire (see Step 8 above) leaving enough material to form a small loop. Then file the end and bend over the wire using fine round-nose pliers. You may pre-bend a loop, leave it open and then slot the wire in before closing the loop.
10. Cut the remaining long wire back, file and bend over the loop. You should now have both wire ends tucked away in a double loop-'knot'.

To make the ear pieces:
1. Straighten and cut two equal lengths of 0.6 mm silver wire (90 mm/3 1/2 in. long).
2. File the ends.
3. Bend a small loop at one end.
4. Round off and polish the other end.
5. Use round nose pliers to grip the silver wire approximately in the middle and bend it down to form a 'U'. The radius of the curve must be big enough to allow the wire to fit easily through the pierced hole so that it will sit comfortably.
6. Open the fine silver loop and hook the 'orbit' spiral into it, then close loop.

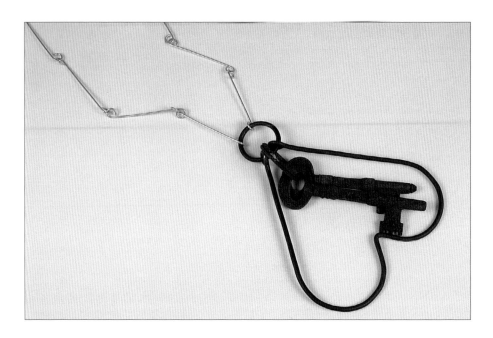

Close 2 My Heart Necklace
(mild steel, silver chain and found objects)

Necklaces offer an ideal platform for uninhibited experimentation and self expression.

To make the heart shapes:

1. Straighten some annealed 1.8 mm or 2 mm (1/16 in.) thick wire of your choice. Clamp in a vice and pull.
2. Use side cutters to cut a length of approximately 230 mm (9 in.).
3. Mark out the centre of the length.
4. Grip the length so that one side of the flat-nosed pliers touches the centre

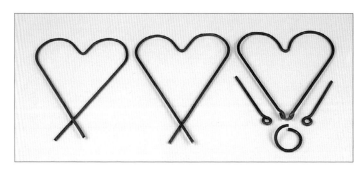

Forming the hearts

mark, and then kink the wire so that it forms a 60° pointed V-shape.

5. Use a round pin which is roughly the size of one heart cheek and shape the wire to form a heart.

6. Trim the wires with either side- or top-cutters so they are equal length and file the ends flat using a flat hand file.

7. Use round-nose pliers to form loops at either ends of the heart straights. Centre the loops and make sure that the loops lie flat and that the openings either both face outwards or inwards.

8. Use another round pin to make a single ring to hold all the parts of the necklace together. The size is up to you, but make sure that the ring is big enough. Cut and file the ends. Do not close it yet.

To make the chain:

1. Straighten a length of 1250 mm (50 in.) of 1 mm or 1.2 mm ($1/16$ in.) thick annealed wire.

2. Cut the length into 20 equal parts (60 mm/$2^{1/4}$ in. each).

3. File the ends.

4. Bend the loops using round-nosed pliers at either ends. Make sure that the links lie flat.

5. Hook the links together. Use flat-nosed pliers to open and close the loops. You determine the final length of the chain; you may have to omit or add some links to suit your taste.

6. Assemble the necklace: heart, found objects and chain, using the still-open single ring. Close the ring.

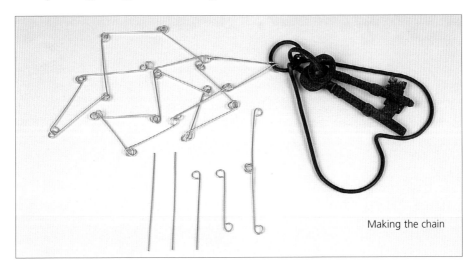

Making the chain

Venus Ring (mild steel wire, silver and pearl)

I originally made this ring as an edition for an exhibition at Gallery 'a' in Geneva, Switzerland. The mild steel wire is untreated and will rust over time, discolouring

parts of the pearl. My intention was to let nature take its course and influence the final outcome over time. I did, of course, tell the customer this and they loved the idea. I have subsequently sold more than 100 of these rings, all of them slightly different as a result of their 'freestyle' feel and appearance.

Use annealed wire. If you want to follow the original design, use a length of about 1000 mm (40 in.) annealed, 1 mm or 1.2 mm (1/16 in.) mild steel wire. Naturally you can use any other annealed wire. There is no need to straighten the wire. Use it as it comes.

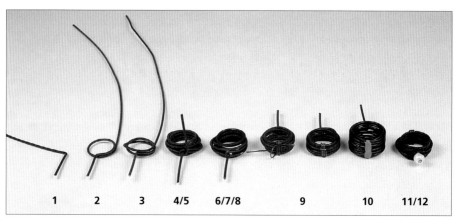

1   2   3   4/5   6/7/8   9   10   11/12

1. Measure 40 mm (1¹/₂ in.) from one end and bend 90° up using flat-nosed or parallel pliers.
2. Choose a pin the size of your ring finger.
3. Wrap the wire around the pin passing the vertical 400 mm (16 in.) wire end underneath three or four times.

56

Step **3**

Step **4**

Step **5**

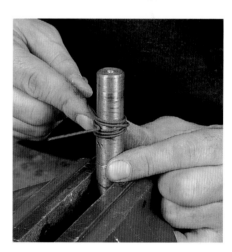

Step **6**

4. Wrap the wire round another three or four times, this time so the wire passes the top of the 40 mm wire end.
5. You will have to change the wire over at the bottom of the ring. The vertical end should now be in the middle of the ring.
6. Continue to wrap the wire around, passing the centre end alternatively from bottom and top until you have reached the size of wrapped ring shank that suits you.

Step **9**

7. Wrap the remaining end once round the centre pin to secure the bundled wire.
8. Cut the wire back as close as possible to the wrapped loop.
9. To hold the bottom part of the ring shank together you can either wrap some fine wire around the bundled wire or you can solder it together.
10. Make a fine silver ring with an inner hole diameter the same size as the thickness of the ring shank wire. Slot it on to the centre pin.
11. Glue a drilled pearl on top of the silver ring. Use either Araldite Rapid or Super Glue. With Araldite you have more time to manoeuvre the pearl around than with Super Glue which only takes about 10 seconds to set. In either case make sure that the glue has fully cured before cutting and filing the centre pin back so it sits flush with the pearl.

Making a Brooch: a little bending exercise

Brooch (mild steel, spraypainted, dental steel pin, white gold ring)

I designed this brooch especially for this book. The various stages look more demanding than they actually are. It may be worthwhile spending some time studying the image of the final brooch to try and visualise what the piece looks like in 3-D.

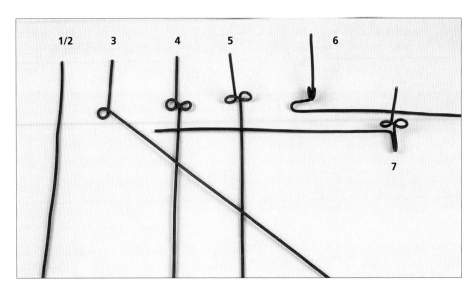

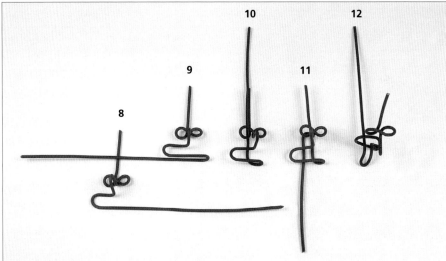

To make the main part of the brooch:

1. Cut a length of 1-1.2 mm (¹/₁₆ in.) wire, in this case I used annealed mild steel wire.

2. Straighten it.

3. Start to form the face 70 mm (2³/₄ in.) away from one end using round-nosed pliers. You will need some material to hold the brooch pin.

4. Bend a double loop to form a horizontal figure of eight. These form the eyes.

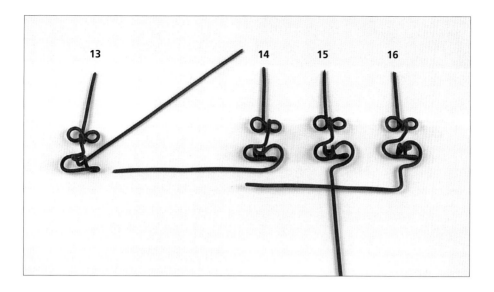

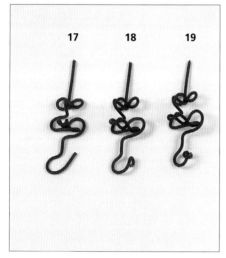

5. Grip the horizontal figure of eight (eyes) including the 70 mm (2¾ in.) end and bend it 90° so the long wire protrudes, then form the nose.

6. Shape the rest of the face following the examples opposite and above (steps 6 to 19).

To make the brooch pin:

I used 0.8 mm thick dental wire. The material and size proved to be successful. The pins are flexible but strong and in general tend to cause least damage to fabrics. If you prefer, you can also use hard-drawn silver wire of the same size

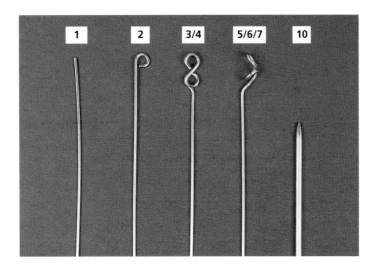

Stages of making
the brooch pin

which will be just as good but easier to form. Do not heat the hard-drawn wire as it will loose its springiness and strength (in effect you would anneal it) required for a brooch pin.

1. Cut a length of wire, longer than the actual brooch, and file one end.
2. Bend a small-sized loop.
3. Bend a second loop to form a figure of eight.
4. Centre the double loop.
5. Kink the double loop (you should be able to slot the double loop on to the brooch end).
6. Bend back the pin so the brooch pin runs parallel to the brooch.
7. Cut the pin back.
8. Shape the end using a fine file and wet and dry paper (this is a type of emery paper for metal). The pin point should be sharp but bullet shaped, rather than a sharp point. The point of the pin should not cut the fibre of the fabric as that would result in a hole, it should instead part the fibre when entering the cloth. The pin point must be polished to run through the fabric smoothly.

To spraypaint the brooch

I suggest that you spraypaint the brooch before you secure the brooch pin. It makes the masking off and other detailing easier.

1. Mask off either end of the brooch using proper masking tape.
2. Clean the surface so that it is free from grease and dust.
3. Apply a thin coat of spraypaint primer. It is better to apply a number of

thin coats of paint rather than one thick coat. Thick coats of spraypaint will run and adhere less well to the surface than layers of thin coats. Make sure that each layer is dry before applying the next coat.

4. Let the primer dry thoroughly. Always allow it to dry overnight to avoid any unpleasant surprises when applying the final coloured coats of spraypaint.
5. Apply the final coloured coats of spraypaint. Two thin coats should be enough.
6. Let the final coat dry thoroughly.

To secure the brooch pin at the top:
1. Move the brooch pin as close as possible to the 'eyes'.
2. Cut back excessive wire (you need about 10-12 mm/$^1/_3$-$^1/_2$ in.) of wire to form a small loop) and file it.
3. Bend a small loop using round-nosed pliers but do not close it up completely yet.
4. Leave a small slot to move the brooch pin back into the loop.
5. Close the loop using parallel pliers.

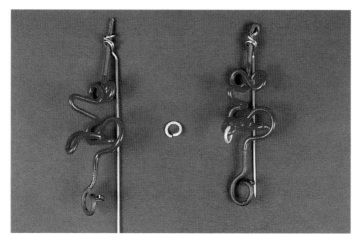

Adding the tongue ring

To make the tongue ring:
Using a metal of your own choice, bend a small tongue ring, either using round-nosed pliers or a small drill or fine pin and carefully slot it on to the tongue. Make sure you do not scratch the paint.

6

Wire artists

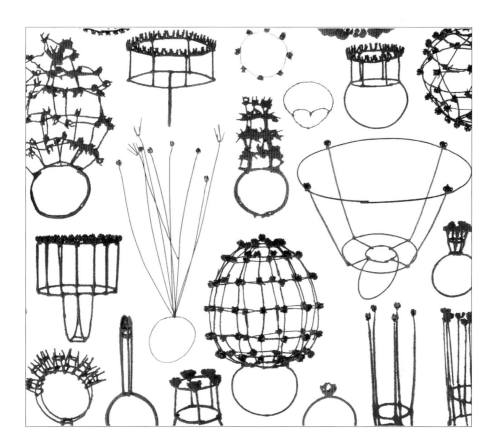

Above:
Bettina Dittlmann (see p.81): *Ringchen* (*Little Rings*), 2002/2003 (iron, enamel, garnet and pyrite). Very fine steel wire has been soldered together to form ring objects so fine that they appear like drawings in space. Some of these ring objects have been encrusted with specks of garnet and pyrite before being coated in layers of powdered enamel. (Photo: Jank/Dittlmann)

Opposite:
Doris Betz (see p.85): *Chain*, 1994 (fine steel wire [binding wire]). The individual links of this chain are based on a traditional manufactured 'loop-in-loop' gold or silver chain. However, here the individual links are not made out of 'solid' wire links. On closer inspection you can see that the individual volume of each link has been created out of wrapped fine binding wire before being linked together to form a 'solid' looking chain. (Photo: D.B.)

Bernhard Schobinger

The Swiss-born artist Bernhard Schobinger is one of the most stimulating and innovative artists working today. He has elevated jewellery as an expressive medium to new levels. His work is often highly political and subversive. Although trained and highly skilled, he uses a deliberate non-skilled approach to challenge perceptions and the notion of value. Wire figures very strongly in Schobinger's work. He often uses precious metals in an immediate and almost untamed way. This direct, uninhibited approach to jewellery-making gives his work intense energy.

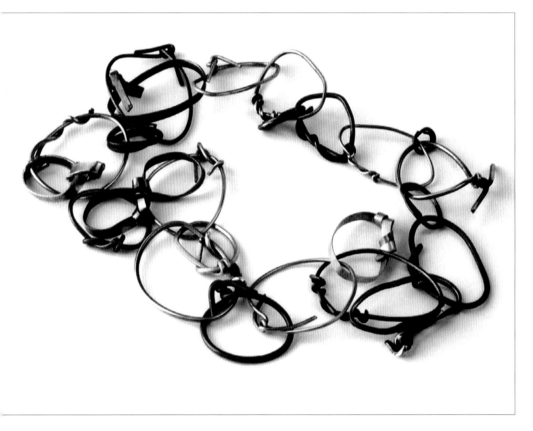

Drahtkette (wire necklace) 1988. Necklace made out of round and square sectioned wires in gold, silver, copper, platinum and tantalum, shaped by hand. (Photo: B.S.)

David Bielander

David Bielander's work is never what it appears to be. His work is strongly concept driven, with either a story that supports his work, or some other twist. Bielander has the ability to exploit the properties and characteristics of materials very effectively to inject meaning into his objects which challenge perceptions. His statements are quiet, subtle but immensely powerful once you realise what it is you have chosen to wear. For example, the illustrated necklace is attractive and pretty; however, once you discover that the rubber rings in this piece are traditionally used to castrate sheep you may need slightly more courage to adorn yourself with such a potent, though 'harmless' looking, necklace.

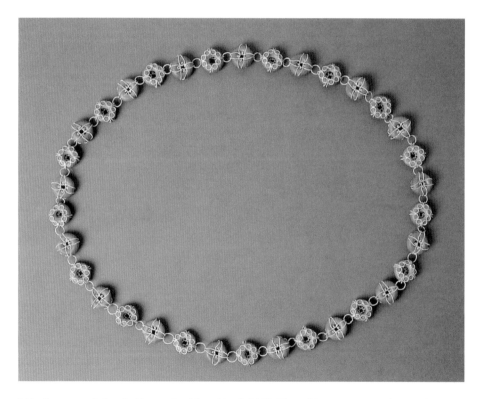

MA pièce a conviction, (rubber and gold necklace), 2002. The gold 'cages' are made out of 0.25 mm thick, almost thread-like wire which has been folded and twisted together to give texture but also strength. Each 'cage' has been soldered or laser welded together individually prior to being assembled into a chain. The rubber rings are then pressed into the empty cages. (Photo: D.B.)

Grosse Brunzbluemli (*Large Pissflowers*), brooches (gold, silver and car body paint), 2003. These brooches have been made out of 0.8 mm square section wire which has been annealed, twisted to create a spiral effect and shaped into one piece. The brooch pin is hard and springy. (Photo: D.B.)

Brunzbluemli (*Pissflowers*), small gold brooches, 2001. These small brooches are formed in the same way as the larger versions of the *Brunzbluemlis* except that the size of the square, sectioned and twisted wire is 0.45 mm. (Photo: D.B.)

Otto Künzli

The Swiss-born and Munich resident artist Otto Künzli is another thinker and maker who has been instrumental in changing the landscape of contemporary jewellery. Trained as a jeweller, he uses his knowledge and experience to produce striking work with meaning based on rigorous concepts and clarity of thought. His conceptual thinking always includes the wearer. This inclusion of the wearer and his understanding of the power of jewellery as a tool for communication make Künzli an outstanding artist.

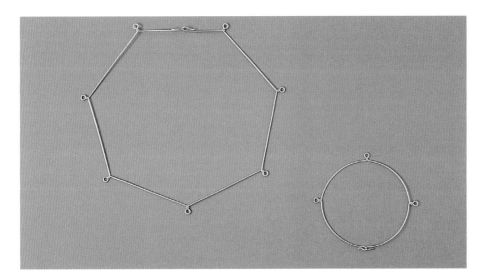

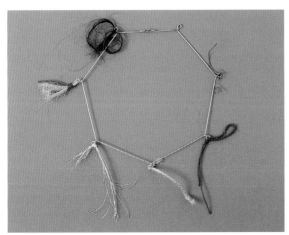

...and you may add whatever you want (gold necklace and bracelet) 2000. These 'diary' pieces were made out of one long, round gold wire. In the necklace, seven small twisted and hammered loops have been formed at each corner of the seven sides, each loop representing one day of the week. You are asked to tie on mementos gathered along the journey of life to 'complete' the piece. In a way, these pieces are contemporary versions of charm bracelets and necklaces worn as a physical reminder of key events and to act as a talisman. (Photo: O.K.)

Jivan Astfalck

Jivan Astfalck's pieces are about the dormant element of objects and materials. It is the things we do not see, the unknown, the seemingly dead, and what emerges after this slumber that is the key to her work. When we sleep, our metabolism slows down, allowing us to rest and to dream. With our eyes shut we are in darkness but we are not dead. Once we open our eyes we are, in a sense, re-born.

Jivan Astfalck was born in Germany and works in the UK.

German oak (necklace - oak, paint and binding wire). Individually painted, German oak twigs have been tied together with thin binding wire, normally used to hold loose parts together during the soldering process, to form a wreath-like neckpiece. (Photo: J.A.)

Bone chain (necklace - fine gold, pearls and chicken bones). The bone sections and the pearls have been strung loosely onto very thin, round fine gold wire lengths. The bone elements and the pearls are able to move along the wire in an abacus manner. These lengths have then been linked together to form one long chain that can either be worn as such or doubled over to create a shorter but 'bushier' necklace. (Photo: J.A.)

Michiyo Tsuzaki

Michiyo Tsuzaki graduated in 2002 with a series of brooches made out of hard-drawn, square-sectioned, soldered silver wire, where the brooch pin became the brooch, therefore moving away from the notion that the brooch has two sides, a front and a back. Michiyo's jewellery consists of well-balanced objects as well as functional brooches.

Left:
Brooch, silver,
(diameter: 70 mm/ 7³/₄ in.), 2002.
(Photo: Bucks University)

Below:
Brooch, silver,
(diameter: 68 mm/ 7³/₄ in.), 2002.
(Photo: Bucks University)

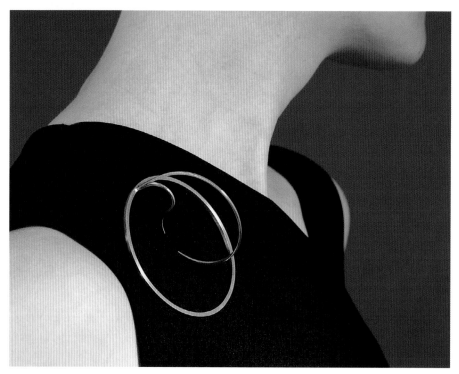

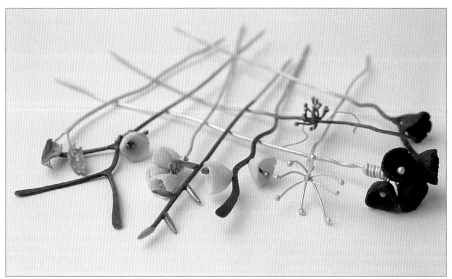

Pins, (silver, gold and porcelain), 2002/2003. These pins have been inspired by the Pre-Raphaelites and their response to nature. Ruth Tomlinson's pins are made out of different-sized silver wires which have been twisted, split, soldered and hammered to emulate 'nature'. Delicate black and white porcelain flowers sit loosely on gold solder adorned stems. (Photo R.T.)

Ruth Tomlinson

Ruth graduated from Manchester Metropolitan University in 2001 in 3-D Design [Jewellery], then did an MA at the Royal College of Art, London, in 2005. Her work and ideas are inspired by materials and processes. Among other things, she is interested in Victorian mourning jewellery, and also in the changing vocabulary of nature and its cycles. She is also fascinated by the 'non-natural' objects that nature hides or reveals, such as the buried treasures of ancient civilisations. Before completing her MA Ruth produced twig-like work using forged and textured precious and non-precious metal wire and incorporating glass, porcelain and other bits and pieces. Since then, she has continued to develop and refine her work using similar raw materials; but now, rather than forging and hammering, she using the process of electroforming to create delicate wire structures embedded with stones, glass and other materials.

This young maker creates pieces of jewellery that are delicate, beautiful and full of small sensitive and lively details that reflect her interests and passion – but most importantly she produces work that you can identify with and that you want to own and live with.

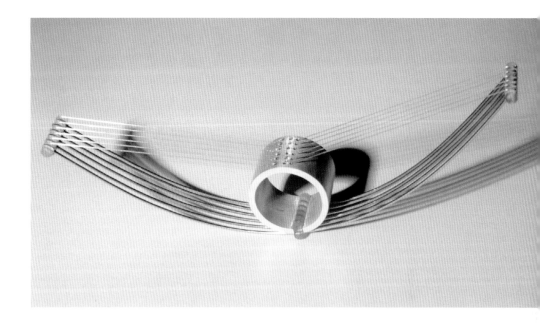

Chris Green

Chris Green's work is about point, line, plane and volume. His interest is in architectural structures, suspension bridges and stringed instruments. Green exploits stainless steel's natural properties and qualities, such as its potential for compression and tension. None of the wires is pre-formed or manipulated. The wires are used in their 'raw' state and are arranged into structures which accentuate the wires' springiness and tension, for example by feeding them through drilled Perspex® spacers or by pulling them together like a bow with taut nylon threads.

Opposite:
Ring (silver, Perspex® and stainless steel wire). A drilled Perspex® spacer is clamped between the split, machined silver ring shank. Six straight stainless steel wires are fed through the drilled, clear Perspex® spacer and bundled together on either end creating a light, dynamic wing-like form. (Photo: C.G.)

Top:
Ring (silver, Perspex®, stainless steel wire and nylon thread). The six stainless steel wires have been pulled together like a bow and are held under tension with nylon threads, which have been secured at the ring shank. (Photo: C.G.)

Andrew Lamb

Andrew Lamb's work is both classic and contemporary. Classic in its appearance, and contemporary in its conceptual use and exploitation of simple materials and processes to create highly sensitive and refined work. The delicate and fluid pieces have been painstakingly constructed from fine twisted precious and non-precious wires. The shimmering, shifting patterns created by this technique echo patterns found in nature but they also remind us of the masterful and fine castwork of ancient civilisations.

Optical necklace (18ct yellow gold wire twisted and soldered), 2001. (Photo: A.L.)

Ikat brooches (silver and copper wire twisted and soldered), 2002. (Photo: A.L.)

Optical pendant (18ct white and yellow gold wire twisted and soldered), 2001. (Photo: A.L.)

Cynthia Cousens

Cynthia Cousens's work is a tribute to the beauty and richness of nature as a source for inspiration and contemplation. Personal observations, impressions and moods are captured and formed into objects of uncluttered simplicity and power. Ideas are 'drawn' directly in materials. Here the artist uses the hammer, the soldering torch and pliers to produce textured and fluid lines in wire, resulting in sensitive, beautiful objects which are testament to a creative inner journey.

Right:
Studies (forged and soldered gold wire). (Photo: Sara Morris)

Below:
Trail (necklace - oxidised, soldered and textured silver wire), 1996. (Photo: Joel Degen)

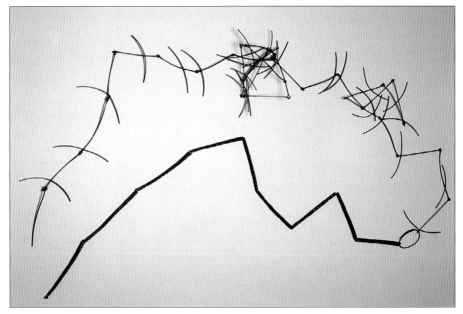

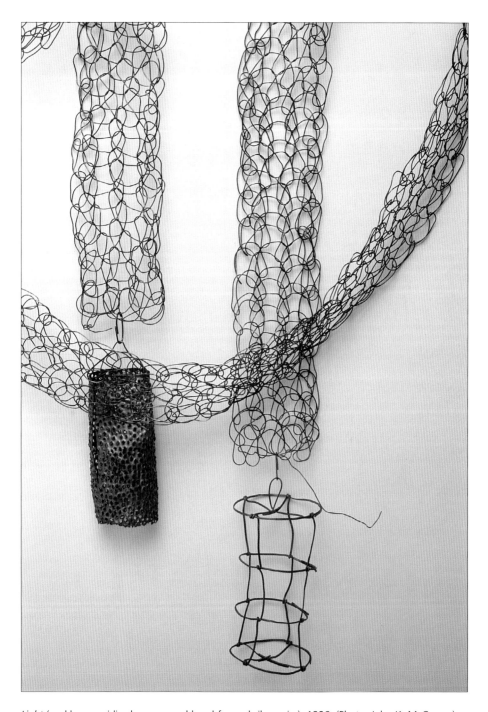

Light (necklace - oxidised, woven and hand-formed silver wire), 1996. (Photo: John K. McGregor)

Mah Rana

The power of Mah Rana's work lies in the fact that she utilises the symbolic potential of her material and use the ritual of making as part of her artistic statement. Her work addresses complex social and psychological issues concerning human conditions and relationships. More recently, her work has explored and examined the importance of owning, giving and wearing jewellery as part of our identity and lives.

Left:
Potential jewellery (gold and steel), 1994. A single pawned wedding ring has been melted and drawn down into gold thread ready to be used. In medieval times the garments of the nobility and the rich were heavily embroidered with precious metal thread and gem stones. (Photo: M.R.)

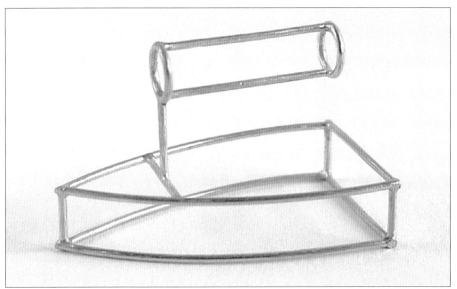

A Woman's Work (gold brooch) 1994. A single, once-used gold wedding ring was purchased, melted and then drawn down into thin, round gold wire, enough to construct (cut and solder) this symbol of domesticity which is both beautiful and charged with meaning. (Photo: M.R.)

His'n'Hers (gold ring) 1995. *His'n'Hers* is made from two pawned wedding rings, one of which is melted down and then reworked into wire (drawn into round wire) to make the cage structure to enclose the other ring.
(Photo: George Meister, *Die Neue Sammlung, Pinakothek der Moderne*, Munich)

Bettina Dittlmann

Imagine a luscious, emerald-green, English lawn wrapped up in morning dew on a beautiful autumn day. This best describes the richness and quality of Bettina Dittlmann's enamelled iron wire jewellery. Her work is like a breath of fresh air that tries to capture the fleeting moments of nature and time. There are not many artists today who possess her technical ability and intuitive understanding of how to fully exploit the potential of wire and powdered enamel in such a powerful and effective way.

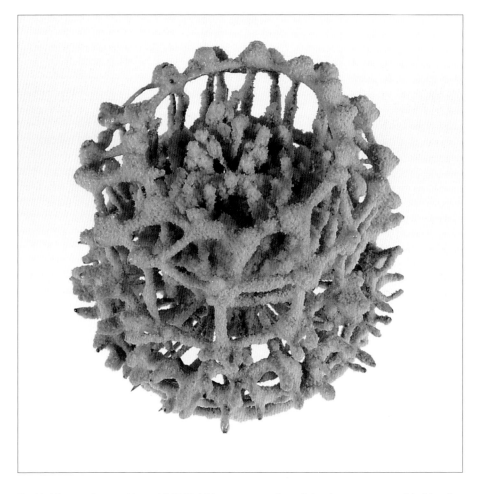

Untitled (iron and enamel brooch) 2000. This sea creature brooch has been constructed (soldered) out of fine-sized steel wire that has been coated with layers of yellow powdered enamel. (Photo: Jank/Dittlmann)

Untitled (brooch), fine iron wire coated with powdered layers of enamel, 1995. This brooch reminds me of a dried flower which time and nature has stripped down to reveal its skeleton structure. (Photo: Jank/Dittlmann)

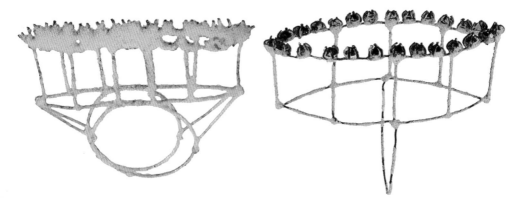

Untitled (yellow jewellery), iron, enamel and garnets, 2001.(Photo: Jank/Dittlmann)

Georg Dobler

Georg Dobler is the Tatlin of constructed wire jewellery. His work, soldered together in fine stainless steel wire, reminds me of work created by the Russian constructivists who, at the beginning of the 20th century, produced dynamic avant-garde work as a tribute to modernity. These geometric and visually precise sculptures defined space, movement and time. They were inspired by modern architecture, the machine and by new materials and technology.

Since his early start as a contemporary jeweller, Dobler has produced an extensive and diverse body of work exploring the potential and possibility of fine architectural, lightweight wire constructions to adorn the body. To make these special constructions he always uses fine 0.6-0.8 mm stainless steel wire. Stainless steel is resilient, strong and can be hard soldered, even when used as thin wire. The final pieces vary in scale, colour and texture. Regardless of their size, the final pieces need to be worn to create a dialogue.

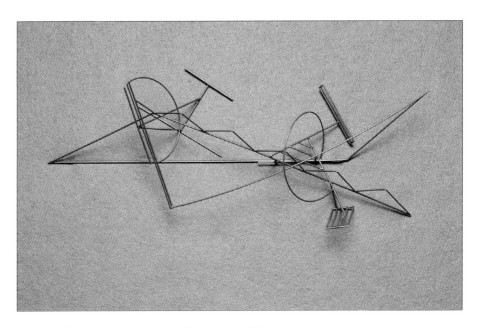

Brooch (soldered and spraypainted stainless steel), 1984.
(Photo: George Meister, *Die Neue Sammlung, Pinakothek der Moderne*, Munich)

Three brooches: Brooch 1 (top), stainless steel, 1987; *Brooch 2* (middle), black chrome-plated stainless steel, 1984; *Brooch 3* (bottom), spraypainted stainless steel, 1983. (Photo: G.D)

Doris Betz

In a short letter to me, Doris Betz raised the importance and potency of wire as a carrier for meaning. She treasures the experience of holding and manipulating wire and the endless possibilities this simple but potent material can offer. Her marks and comments in wire are lively, rich in texture and sensuous. A piece of wire is a physical line in space with a tangible beginning and end. A line is a journey and a symbol for life and death. She says: 'It is what happens in between, the journey from one end to the other which interests and fascinates me.' Her work in wire provides some answers as to what can be discovered on this journey.

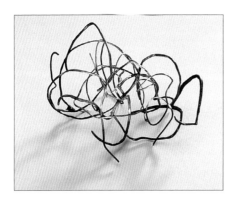

Left:
Brooch, 1997. Forged, soldered and oxidised silver wires have been formed freely into a cloud-like brooch.
(Photo: George Meister, *Die Neue Sammlung, Pinakothek der Moderne*, Munich)

Below:
Pendants, 1994. Fine steel (binding wire) and fine silver wire have been wrapped around a ring to build up volume and weight.
(Photo: D.B.)

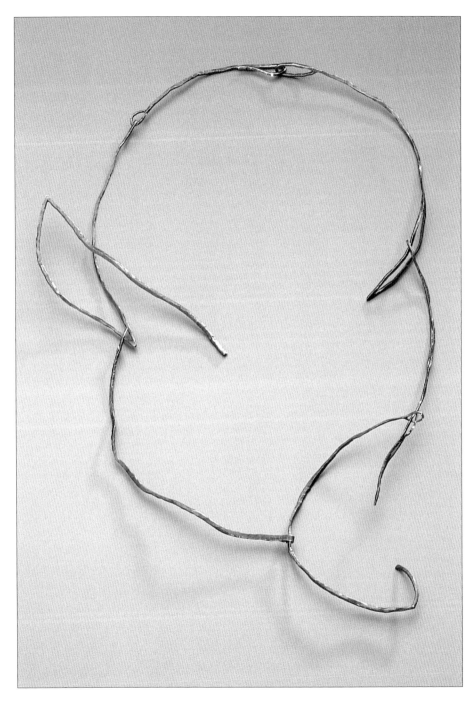

Necklace, 1997. Forged, oxidised silver wire elements are linked together to form a chain with irregular links. (Photo: George Meister, *Die Neue Sammlung, Pinakothek der Moderne*, Munich)

Baule Tribe, Ghana

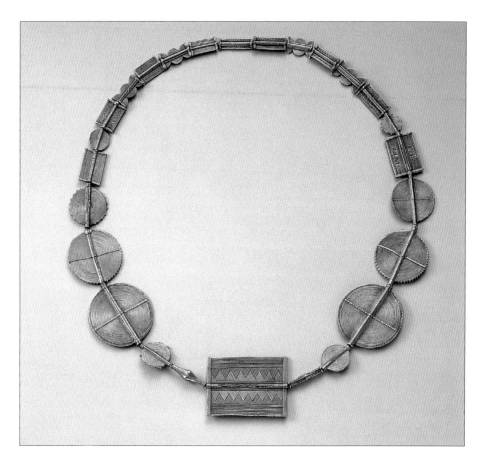

Necklace (cast fine gold and various gold alloys), Baule, Ghana, Côte d'Ivoire. This necklace was initially constructed out of wire, thin wax threads and then cast in gold. (Photo: George Meister, *Die Neue Sammlung, Pinakothek der Moderne*, Munich)

The necklace pictured above was made in the first half of 20th century. Fine wire-like strands of wax were used to build the 'master', which was then packed into clay, fired and cast. Each piece was original.

The Baule people are famous for using this intricate lost-wax casting technique similar to that of their ancestors the Ashanti, who used this lost-wax casting process 300 years ago. Today they inhabit Ghana and Côte d'Ivoire.

Vivianna Torun Bulow-Hube

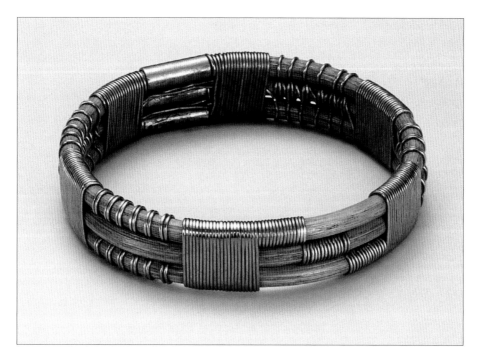

Bracelet (wicker reed coiled and bound with brass wire and tube), 1948.
(Photo: George Meister, *Die Neue Sammlung, Pinakothek der Moderne*, Munich)

Born in 1929 in Malmo, Sweden, Vivianne Torun Bulow-Hube died in 2004 in Jakarta, Indonesia. She trained as a goldsmith and silversmith in Stockholm, lived and worked in France and Germany, and finally established roots in Jakarta where she worked until her death. She was a jewellery designer and silversmith who helped to influence a number of emerging artists and designers who came out of Scandanavia. She designed collections for George Jensen and collaborated with Picasso, Braque, Miro, Alexander Calder and many more.

Wolfgang Tümpel

The jeweller, designer, politician and teacher, Wolfgang Tümpel was born in 1903 in Bielefeld, Germany. He was an influential and inspiring teacher who was also a committed lighting designer. He trained as a jeweller in 1921 and became a protégé of Dr Hans Prinzhorn, the famous psychiatrist who wrote the seminal book *Bildnerei der Geisteskranken (The Art of the Insane)*. Prinzhorn was one of the first to recognise that there was barely a difference between the 'sane' and the 'insane' artist in terms of artistic drive and the need for self expression. In 1922 Wolfgang Tümpel decided to complete his studies as a jeweller and designer at the Bauhaus in Weimar where he was taught by Paul Klee, Laszlo Moholy-Nagy and Oskar Schlemmer. Throughout his life he continued to design lights for industry, make jewellery and teach. He died in 1978.

Necklace (fine gold wire). 38 almost identical components have been coiled like springs and linked together into this simple but beautiful chain. This is an excellent example of an intelligent and resourceful use of materials and skills. (Photo: George Meister, *Die Neue Sammlung, Pinakothek der Moderne*, Munich)

Hermann Jünger

Every discipline needs its rebels and heroes who are instrumental in revolutionising and expanding its boundaries. It is their mission to question convention, tear down perceptions and find new ways of voicing their opinions. They clear the table and open the floodgates as artists and inspiring teachers so that new talent can follow and invariably help to contribute and shape the new emerging landscape. The German artist Hermann Jünger is one such rebel.

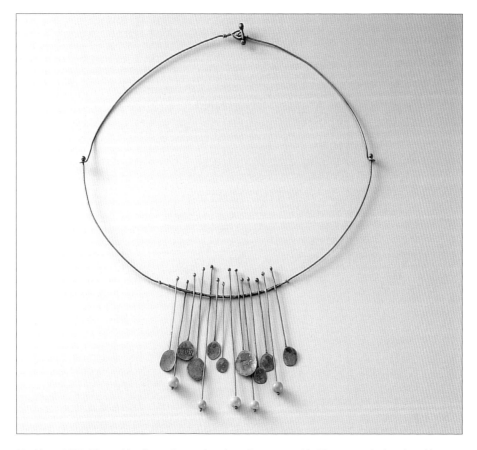

Necklace, 1958. Three thin silver wire sections have been assembled into an articulated necklace. 14 vertical lengths have been soldered onto the bottom section. Some ends have been adorned with turquoise beads, others with spoon-shaped elements which have been soldered onto the fine, vertical wire rays. Note the way the neck wire segments have been joined. Most of the wire ends were melted to form little pin heads. This softens the ends and prevents the moving beads from falling off, but most importantly it gives this simple, graceful piece an understated beauty. (Photo: George Meister, *Die Neue Sammlung, Pinakothek der Moderne*, Munich)

91

Manfred Bischoff

Manfred Bischoff is one of the great contemporary goldsmiths of Europe. He is an artist and craftsman with a unique creative vision. The jewellery he creates is mostly made from precious materials. His pieces are sensual, lyrical and beautifully executed with a sharp eye for detail and a refined understanding of materials. His work seems perceptively simple but the beauty often masks a ferocious irony and satire.

His jewellery, though highly artistic and meaningful in its own right, is always about adornment, and needs the body of the wearer to reveal its full 'personality'. Manfred Bischoff was born in 1947, studied at the *Fachhochschule Pforzheim*, Munich. He worked in Berlin before moving to Tuscany, where he still lives and works.

Brooch (spraypainted stainless steel wire). The brooch pin and fixing has been attached to the vertical arm. The message 'Nein' has been bent in one continuous line before being soldered on to the vertical arm. This brooch is a good example of jewellery used as a tool for communication. (Photo: Eva Junger, *Die Neue Sammlung, Pinakothek der Moderne*, Munich)

Herman Hermsen

For more than 20 years Herman Hermsen has been part of the *avant garde* as a jeweller, designer and teacher. He has produced a unique body of work that is underpinned by rigorous conceptual thinking and which has been realised with precision and skill. The minimalist beauty of his work provokes thought and requires a committed wearer.

As Paul Derrez, founder and owner of the influential Jewellery Gallery RA in Amsterdam says: 'What makes Herman Hermsen's work so surprising - his jewellery and other pieces - is their utilitarian character. Everything has been thought through and has a reason. With their restrained design, perfect function and finesse of detail, Herman's pieces have become great favourites and potential classics.'

Brooch (stainless steel, bent at either end and spraypainted yellow), 1983. Herman Hermsen's brooch is brooch and pin all in one. The piece has been stripped down to the bare minimum. What remains is the essence or idea of a brooch. All you will get is a dynamic, yellow flash, a signal or mark. With minimalist pieces such as this brooch, attention to detail is absolutely crucial. The bent ends define the beginning and the end but they also give the piece volume and energy. The kinked ends also make the brooch wearable. To fasten the brooch you flex the 'pin' and grip the fabric at either end, then relax the pin.
(Photo: Eva Junger, *Die Neue Sammlung, Pinakothek der Moderne*, Munich)

Vaclav Cigler

Vaclav Cigler is a renowned glass artist who was only involved in jewellery for a while, but what he did during that short time left a profound mark on the development and voice of contemporary European jewellery. He designed a series of extravagant jewels in gold, stainless steel and plastic which he described as *Spielerei (Playing)*. Although his work has a humorous and playful edge, the pieces do challenge the notion of ornament, wearability and purpose, and the role of jewellery as a commodity.

Vaclav Cigler was born in 1929 and lives and works in Prague.

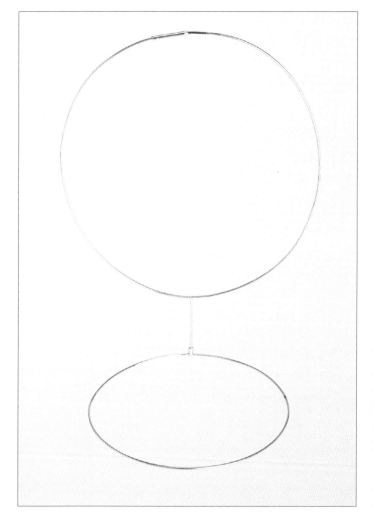

Head/face adornment (brass chrome plated). Two simple rings which can be adjusted. The larger ring is worn like a head band with the smaller one folded so it 'frames' the face. (Photo: Eva Junger, *Die Neue Sammlung, Pinakothek der Moderne*, Munich)

Patrick Muff

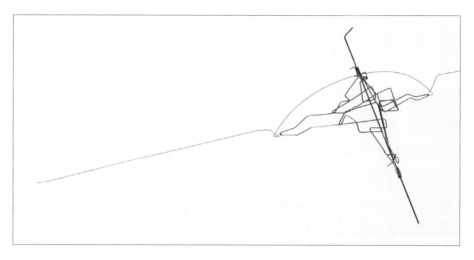

Brooch (fine binding wire and steel). This most delicate piece has been constructed out of four parts in very fine mild steel binding wire. It has been formed and joined by clever bending without any soldering into a cross with a figure 'trapped' in its centre. The top bar of the cross acts as the brooch pin. The pin can be pushed through the two coiled, spring elements on either end of the cross bar. Due to its delicate nature, this brooch is not a piece that is intended to be worn on a daily basis. (Photo: Eva Junger, *Die Neue Sammlung, Pinakothek der Moderne*, Munich)

When we look at the work of Patrick Muff, born in 1962 in Hochdorf in Switzerland, we get a sense that we already know it - or at least that we have seen it somewhere before. He uses the shapes and iconographical programme of the trivial repertory of the Hell's Angels. He uses the familiar and trivial to make ornaments that, on closer inspection, reveal powerful objects that could be inspired by occultism. He loves words and their power to give a piece an identity; each brooch, ring and pendant bears an engraved text that gives his work a mysterious dimension. Patrick Muff now lives and works in Cologne.

Johanna Dahm

Johanna Dahm created a whole range of brooches which, when twisted into the cloth, shaped and manipulated the fabric into 'jewellery'. These brooches or shaped pins became a means to an end by turning the fabric – traditionally only the 'carrier' or the background – into the jewel.

Brooch (aluminium anodised black), 1981.
(Photo: Eva Junger, *Die Neue Sammlung, Pinakothek der Moderne*, Munich)

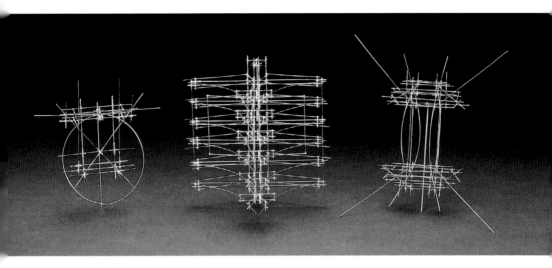

Series of three brooches (fine stainless steel soldered). All three brooches have been constructed out of very fine stainless steel wire which has been soldered together into these complex, spiky and futuristic looking objects. The solder joints have been deliberately left raw. (Photo: George Meister, *Die Neue Sammlung, Pinakothek der Moderne*, Munich)

Andreas Treykorn

The proverb 'no rose without a thorn' fully captures the characteristics of Andreas Treykorn's work made in fine stainless-steel wire. Andreas Treykorn sees his fine, delicate but prickly jewellery constructions as three-dimensional drawings in space. His objects are both charming for their balance and disturbing for their needle-like endings.

Andreas Treykorn was born in Berlin in 1960. He trained as a traditional goldsmith and studied jewellery at the *Fachhochschule* in Cologne. He has been exhibiting his work since 1987. In 1988 he received the Herbert Hoffmann Prize in Munich. Since 1991 he has had his own gallery where he promotes both his own work and that of other contemporary jewellers. He lives and works in Berlin.

Giovanni Corvaja

Brooch (fine gold, silver and white gold wire woven into a square pad), 1990.
(Photo: George Meister, *Die Neue Sammlung, Pinakothek der Moderne*, Munich)

Giovanni Corvaja is a jeweller who graduated from the famous Goldsmith School of Padua, which teaches the high art of making fine contemporary jewellery in predominantly precious metals. These artisans are also proud to prepare and make all the 'raw' materials themselves including their own precious metal alloys. Thus, each maker will be recognised through their work and the colour of their alloy. It is said that Giovanni Corvaja possesses the skills of an angel, which is why he is able to produce work of such great visual and technical complexity.

Brune Boyer-Pellerej

Brooch 'Message' (brass, gold-leafed and welded), 1992. At first glance the true value and content of this intriguing piece is not obvious. On closer inspection you can see that the irregular texture of the brooch is built up out of words formed in wire in one continuous line. The words or sentences were gold-leafed before they were coiled and welded together to form this sensuous, tactile circular wire pad. What, we ask ourselves, is the secret message concealed within? We will never know, but its secret will continue to tease our curiosity. This is its power and true value. (Photo: George Meister, *Die Neue Sammlung, Pinakothek der Moderne*, Munich)

Brune Boyer-Pellerej was born in Toulouse in 1967. She studied jewellery design from 1985-1990 at the *École Supérieure des Arts Appliqués* in Geneva. In 1993 she moved to Spain where she worked and promoted her work before moving back to Paris in 1997. Brune Boyer-Pellerej has shown her work in galleries throughout Europe. Her work can be found in private and public collections such as the *Danner-Stiftung* in Munich.

Thomas Detlef

In the south of France you often come across churches with flat-roofed towers. The flat roof is adorned with a separate transparent wrought-iron structure, simulating the more traditional tiled, pointed and steeped roof which houses the church bells. The richness and ornamentation of these transparent bell roofs depends on the wealth of the particular village or town. Thomas Detlef's transparent, baroque, pendant constructed in square sectioned silver wire reminds me of one of these 'bell roofs'.

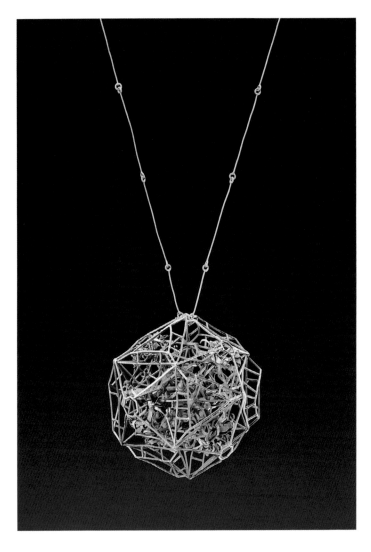

Necklace (square-sectioned gold and oxidised silver wire construction soldered into a facetted 'ball'), 1988. Amongst this dense architectural grid one will discover small laurels, gold ribbons and other details with historic references. These details are there as an invitation and a catalyst for thought. (Photo: George Meister, *Die Neue Sammlung, Pinakothek der Moderne*, Munich)

Necklace (square-sectioned silver wire soldered together and oxidised), 1989. (Photo: Eva Junger, *Die Neue Sammlung, Pinakothek der Moderne*, Munich)

Volker Atrops

I first came across the work of Volker Atrops when I was searching through the archive and collection of the *Danner-Stiftung* in Munich (now housed in *Die Neue Sammlung, Pinakothek der Moderne*, Munich). I know very little about this artist but I instantly fell in love with the set of aluminium rings shown below; their raw energy, simplicity and immediacy cast a powerful spell. They appear to have been knotted on the spot. The ends of the profiled square aluminium wire are just cut off with side cutters and deliberately left as they are. It is this detail that gives the pieces their power. What he has produced are multiples with an individual touch. Here is someone who has an intuitive understanding of a material and its potential and who has utilised this to express an idea with *chutzpah*.

Seven rings (facetted, sandblasted aluminium), 1993. The seven rings are part of an edition. They have been formed out of a pre-fabricated, facetted soft aluminium wire on the spot, quickly and intuitively. The ends have been deliberately left raw and unfinished. This rough and ready quality and the fluent energetic knots form the strength and beauty of the pieces. They challenge the notion of skill, labour and the value of artistic expression of the custom-made object. Volker Atrops' rings are a comment and a possible answer to all the rather bland and unimaginative bent wire objects offered for sale on the street, or at market stalls or fun-fairs. (Photo: George Meister, *Die Neue Sammlung, Pinakothek der Moderne*, Munich)

E.R. Nele

The artist, sculptress and jeweller Eva Renee Nele (or E.R. Nele as she prefers to be known) was born in 1932 in Berlin, the daughter of the future founder of the *Documenta* – one of the biggest international contemporary art shows, held every 4-5 years in Kassel. Her early childhood was spent in Kassel. She studied at the Central School of Arts and Crafts in London, at the *Hochschule fuer Bildende Kunst* in Berlin and the *Atelier Lacouriere* in Paris. The central theme in E.R. Nele's *oeuvre* is '*der Mensch*' ('Humans'). Through her sculptures and drawings she tries to visualise and record man's emotional and physical condition. Wearing jewellery for her is an important part of the human condition, and explains why she has always made jewellery for people.

E.R. Nele has been awarded many prestigious prizes. She has exhibited her work extensively in her native Germany and internationally and her work is represented in major museums and collections worldwide. Since 1965, E.R. Nele has been based in Frankfurt, Germany.

Necklace with removable pendant (18ct gold wire soldered and constructed), 1959. The necklace is a dense mesh of thin gold wires soldered and woven together into a delicate looking, richly textured and flexible web. The triangular part at the front of the necklace can be removed and worn as a pendant. (Photo: George Meister, *Die Neue Sammlung, Pinakothek der Moderne*, Munich)

Hans Stofer

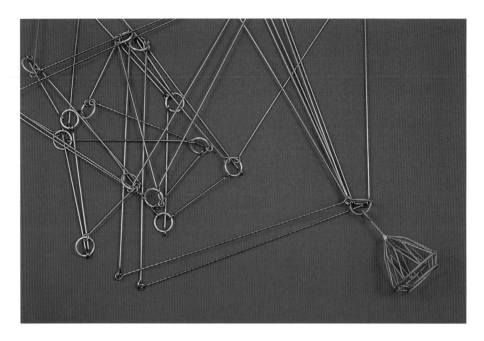

Diamond necklace (spot welded mild steel skeleton of a diamond suspended from a stainless steel web-like chain), 2000. (Photo: H.S.)

When I was a boy, I believed that a cherry tree would grow with its own face if I carved a face into a cherry stone and planted that stone into the soil. Forty-two years later I know that those who told me this was impossible were wrong.

I was born 47 years ago in Switzerland. I had no idea what I wanted to be when I grew up so I went to school and did all that was expected of me. I decided to become an artist because I was tired of being told what to do. Now, although most of the time I do not know what I am doing, I am happy that I can get up in the morning, look into the mirror and get on with the day. We have been in London since 1987. I make stuff, teach, write a bit, and make some more stuff. The country scares me but I love London, Caroline, the kids, the cat, and all the bugs in the house. I miss the mountains though.

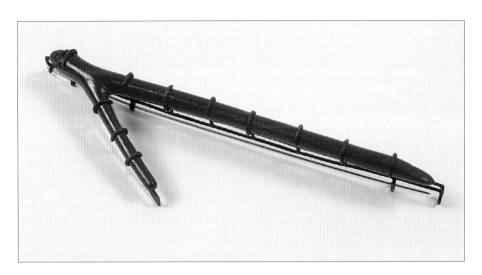

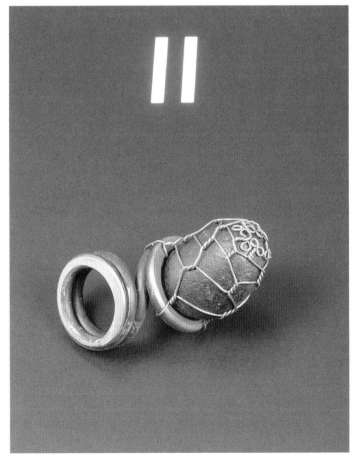

Above:
Twig brooch (mild steel spot-welded, with a lacquered twig), 1990. (Photo: H.S.)

Left:
Pebbledash ring, 2001, coiled thick mild steel ring shank where one end has been bent 90° upwards to provide the base for the setting of the pebble. The egg-shaped pebble has been tied into position with fine mild steel binding wire. (Photo: H.S.)

Glossary

Alloy a metallic material consisting of a mixture of two or more metals or metallic elements.

Anneal to soften metal by heating.

Binding wire thin, soft wire usually in mild steel used to bind or hold parts together.

Blowtorch an apparatus that burns with a hot flame for welding, soldering or brazing.

Braze to join metal with brass (like soldering).

Bright steel ground or polished steel sheet, rod or wire

Burnish to smooth and polish a metal surface using a burnisher (special polishing tool).

Casting the process of transferring molten metal into a mould.

De-bur to remove sharp edges from metal after cutting or drilling, either using a file or a special de-burring tool.

Dental steel a special steel alloy otherwise used for medical/dental purposes. This steel is tough and does not corrode or cause allergic reactions.

Draw either to make profiled wire, rod or tube or to reduce its size by pulling through a drawplate. Can also refer to making wire longer by hammering it.

Drawbench a machine used to draw either round or profiled wire, or tube, down to size. Also used to pull and straighten soft wire.

Drawplate hardened steel plate used to reduce the diameter of wire by drawing it through conical holes, either by hand or using a draw bench.

Ductile malleable enough to be drawn out into wire, rolled, stretched or hammered into thin sheets.

Electroform to form a metal object by eletrolytic deposition on an armature, matrix or mould. A conductive paint must first be applied.

Electroplating to coat metal with metal by electrolysis.

Enamelling to inlay, coat or otherwise decorate metal with a coloured, translucent or opaque glassy substance which is fused together in a heated kiln.

Etching wearing away the surface of metal, glass, etc., by chemical action using acid.

Fibula a metal pin resembling a safety pin.

Ferrous iron-based metals.

File a hand-tool used for shaping and smoothing metals and other materials.

Flux a substance used to prevent oxidisation during the soldering process.

Forge a hearth or furnace used for heating metal.

Former a tool for giving a coil or a winding a required shape.

Fuse Join metal through heat and pressure.

Galvanise in particular to cover iron or steel with a protective zinc coating by dipping it into molten zinc or by electro-deposition.

Gauge an instrument for measuring.

Grind Reduce or shape using a power tool such as an angle grinder or a special table-mounted tool grinder.

Ingot piece of cast metal usually obtained from a mould in a suitable form for further use.

Jig a simple tool to produce repetitive shapes or forms.

Lustre the sheen, gloss or shine of metal or other materials once they have been polished.

Malleable can be shaped or bent without breaking, a characteristic that allows us to bend, twist or compress metals or other materials.

Mandrel a much larger tapered tool used to shape rings.

Mild steel any of a class of steel that contains a low quantity of carbon. This steel will rust.

Non-ferrous metals that are not iron-based, i.e., copper, brass, aluminium, etc.

Oxidise to form or cause to form a layer or metal on another, when the first mteal is exposed to air, e.g., rust on steel.

Patinate to artificially oxidise/change the colour of metal surfaces using either heat or chemicals.

Pierce to saw using a special saw and fine piercing saw blades.

Plannish to flatten or smooth out metal surfaces using a special hammer and hammering technique.

Precious metals siler, gold, platinum, etc.

Propane a colourless flammable gas used as fuel or for heating metals, etc.

Rolling mill a machine with flat or shaped rollers used to reduce ingots to produce small sheets or bars.

Sandblasting to clean, grind, or decorate a surface using a jet of sand or grit blown from a nozzle under air or steam pressure.

Setting to set stones of other objects into a special metal mount.

Solder to join metals by heating and introducing an alloy.

Spot-welder a tool to fuse two pieces of, usually ferrous, metals together using electrically generated heat and pressure.

Spring steel very hard stainless-steel alloy used to make springs.

Stainless steel a type of steel resistant to corrosion as a result of the presence of large amounts of chromium.

Tarnish a form of oxidisation. Used predominantly in connection with non-ferrous and precious materials.

Tin plate thin steel sheet coated with tin.

Tongs a pliers-like tool for grasping, usually hot, materials.

Triblett a small tapered tool used to make small links or rings.

Vice tool with a pair of jaws that close with a lever or a screw; used to hold an object immobile while it is being worked on.

Weld to join metal with the same material.

Suppliers

Precious metal wire:

ARGEX Ltd
130 Hockley Hill
Birmingham B18 5AN
0121 248 4344
email: silver@argex.co.uk

Cooksen & Exchange Findings
49 Hatton Garden, The City
London EC1N 8YS
020 7400 6500

Rashbel
24-28 Hatton Wall, London EC1 8JH
020 7831 5646
email: orders@rashbel.com

Dental steel wire:
Scientific Wire Co
18 Raven Road, London E18 8HW
020 8504 3332

Ferrous and Non-ferrous metal wire:
Fays Metals Ltd
Unit 1, 37 Colville Road
Alton W3 8BL
020 8993 8883

Jewellery tools and equipment
Walsh Brothers
118-120 High Street
Beckenham
Kent BR3 1EB
020 8650 4001

Ruth Tomlinson. *Brooch* from 'Hoard', made of glass, silver and gold using electroforming.

Places to view wire jewellery

BELGIUM
Galerie Sofie Lachaert, Tilrode. www.lachaert.com

GERMANY
Dannerstiftung, Pinakothek der Moderne, Munich. www.pinakothek.de

THE NETHERLANDS
Galerie MARZEE, Nijmegen. www.marzee.nl

SWITZERLAND
Galerie SO, Solothurn. www.galerieso.com

Galerie TACTILE, Geneva. www.tactile.ch.

UK
British Museum, London. www.thebritishmuseum.ac.uk

Contemporary Applied Arts, London. www.caa.org.uk

Crafts Council Collection, London. www.craftscouncil.org.uk

V&A Museum, London; Jewellery Room and Ironwork Gallery.
www.vam.ac.uk

USA
Helen Drutt Gallery, 2222 Rittenhouse Square, Philadelphia PA 19103-5505
druttenglish@helendrutt.com

Sienna Gallery, 80 Main Street, Lenox, MA 01240
info@siennagallery.com

Velvet Da Vinci, 2015 Polk Street, San Francisco LA 94109
info@velvetdavinci.com

Bibliography

Alessi, Alberto, *Family Follows Fiction*, Alessi, 1993

Baviera, Silvio, *Feuer Uber Wasser*, Museum Baviera, 1996

Besset, Maurice, *Alexander Calder*, Verlag: Kunsthaus Zurich, 1975

Bovin, Murray, *Jewellery Making*, Murray Bovin Publisher, 1964

Brepohl, *Theorie und Praxis des Goldschmiedes*, Fachbuchverlag Leibzig

Grimwade, Mark, *Precious Metals*, Butterworth & Co (Publishers) Ltd., 1985

Heskett, John, *Toothpicks & Logos*, Oxford University Press, 2002

McGrath, Jinks, *The Encyclopedia of Jewellery Making Techniques*, Headline Book
    Publishing, 1995

Maguire, Mary, *Wirework*, Anness Publishing Limited, 1996

Marchessean, Daniel, *The Intimate World of Alexander Calder*, Harry N
    Abrahams, 1990

Maurer, Ellen, *Taetigkeitsbericht 2000*, Die Neue Sammlung Munchen, 2000

Rana, Mah, *Jewellery is Life*, Fabrica, 2002

Ruskin, John, *On Art And Life*, Penguin Books - Great Ideas, 2004

Slesin, Suzanne, *Wire*, Abbeville Press Publishers, 1994

Untracht Oppi, *Enameling on Metal*, Chilton Company Publishers, 1962

Index

alloy 12, 33, 41, 88, 98
aluminium 96, 102
annealing 17, 18, 19, 30, 32, 33, 34, 51, 60, 68
anodising 96
articulated joints 39, 91
Ashanti 9, 88
Astfalck, Jivan 70
Atrops, Volker 102

bangles 24
base 12
Baule Tribe 88
beads 91
beeswax 19
bench block 26, 27
bench vice 31, 40
bending 17, 33, 59
Berlin 92, 97, 103
'Berlin' jewellery 11
Betz, Doris 65, 86-7
Bielander, David 67-8
binding wire 18, 65, 70, 86, 95, 105
Bischoff, Manfred 92
blowpipe, mouth 41
blowtorch 41
bone 71
Borax 41, 42
Boyer-Pellerej, Brune 99
bracelet 69, 89
brass 12, 14, 18, 20, 41, 44, 45, 89, 94, 99
bronze 9, 10, 12, 49
brooches 12, 59, 60-3, 68, 72, 80, 83, 92, 93, 95-9, 105
Bulow-Hube, Vivianna Torun 89-90

Calder, Alexander 14-5, 89
casting 11, 12, 88
chain 35, 36, 54, 55, 65, 71, 90
China/Chinese 10
chisel 26
chrome 85, 94
chromium 33
Cigler, Vaclav 94
coiling 29, 33
copper 9, 10, 12, 14, 16, 18, 20, 26, 31, 41, 44-6, 49, 66, 77
corroding 16
Corvaja, Giovanni 98
Cousens, Cynthia 78
cutters 23, 53, 55

Dahm, Johanna 96
Danner-Stiftung 99, 102
dental steel 33, 50, 51, 52, 59, 61
Derrez, Paul 93

Detlef, Thomas 100
diamond 104
Dittlmann, Bettina 65, 82-3
Dobler, Georg 84
Documenta 103
drawbench 20
drawing 17, 19
drawplate 13, 19, 20
drawtongs 19, 33
drills 22, 31, 40

earrings 51, 53
electroforming 73
enamel 46, 48, 49, 65, 82, 83

ferrous 12
file/s 21, 22, 24, 25, 26, 27, 34, 52
flux 41, 42, 43, 48
forging 12, 86, 87
formers 16, 21, 28, 30
frit 48

galvanised 13
garnet 65, 83
gas torch 17
G-clamps 31
gemstones 80
glass 48, 73
gold 9, 10, 11, 12, 16, 20, 31, 41, 44, 45, 46, 59, 65, 66, 67, 68, 69, 71, 73, 76, 77, 78, 80, 81, 88, 89, 90, 91, 94, 98, 99, 100, 103
Green, Chris 75

hammer 17, 21, 22, 26, 27, 30, 69, 73, 78
handtorch 42
hardened wire 33
Hermsen, Herman 93
hide 26

iron 11, 12, 13, 46, 65, 82, 83, 100

Jensen, George 89
jig 21, 28
joining 34, 39
Jünger, Hermann 91

kiln 17
Künzli, Otto 69

Lamb, Andrew 76, 77
lacquer 105
lead 12, 18, 26
links 12, 35, 52, 55, 71
loops 12, 34, 52, 53, 55, 58, 60, 62, 63, 65, 69

lustre 16

mallets 28
molybdenum 33
mobiles 14, 15
Muff, Patrick 95

necklaces 50, 52, 54, 64, 66, 67, 69, 70, 71, 76, 77-9, 88, 90, 91, 100-1, 103-4
Nele, E.R. 103
nitric acid 46
non-ferrous 12, 20, 51
non-precious 14, 40
nylon 75

oxidisation 41, 48, 49, 79, 86, 87, 100-1

paint 46, 49, 62, 63, 68, 70
patination 49
pearl 56, 58, 71
pebble 105
pendant 77
Perspex® 38, 75
piano wire 18
piercing saw 22, 27, 28, 35
plastic 14, 26, 29, 94
plating 48
platinum 12, 15, 18, 66
pliers 15, 19, 21-4, 27, 29, 30, 33, 34, 35, 36, 52-56, 60, 63, 78
polishing 16, 45, 46
porcelain 73
Prague 94
precious 12, 20, 40, 51
propane 42, 43
pyrite 65

Rana, Mah 80
rings 2, 8, 35, 56-8, 65, 74, 75, 80, 81, 83, 102, 105
rolling 17
  mill 20
rust 13, 18, 22, 33, 45, 46, 49

sandblasting 46, 102
Schlemmer, Oskar 90
Schobinger, Bernhard 66
silicon 33
silver 9-12, 16, 18, 31, 41, 43-6, 49, 53, 54, 56, 61, 65, 66, 68, 72, 73, 77, 78, 79, 86, 87, 89, 91, 98, 100-1
smelting 9, 11
solder 12, 18, 30, 39, 41,

42, 43, 44, 67, 70, 73, 76, 77, 78, 80, 82, 84, 85, 91, 92, 95, 97, 100-1, 103
spirals 36, 37, 53
spraypaint 47, 59, 62, 63, 84, 85, 92, 93
spring wire 33
springs 35, 39
stabiles 14
steel 8, 11, 14, 26, 44, 45, 80, 82, 84, 85, 86, 95
  cut 11
  mild 13, 18, 45, 49, 51, 53, 54, 56, 59, 60, 104, 105
  stainless 14, 18, 33, 45, 51, 75, 93, 94, 97, 104
  tinned 14
Stofer, Hans 2, 8, 104
stones 73
stove enamelling 49
surface treatments 45
Sweden 89
Switzerland 95, 104

tantalum 66
tarnishing 16, 45, 48, 49
thread 80
tin 41
tinkers 13, 15
titanium 33
Tomlinson, Ruth 73
Treykorn, Andreas 97
Tsuaki, Michiyo 72
Tümpel, Wolfgang 90
twisting 17, 30, 34, 40, 68, 69, 73, 76, 77

vanadium 33
vice 31, 32, 33, 37, 39, 53, 54

wax 46, 88
weaving 79
welding 33, 39, 44, 99
  laser 67
  resistance 44
  spot 44, 45, 105
winding 29
wood 26, 29, 35

Yugoslavia 9

zinc 12, 13